PRAISE FOR LORI BRYANT-WOOLRIDGE AND
THE POWER OF WOW

"Woolridge comes on like Judith Krantz with a social conscience."

—*Publishers Weekly*

"Busyness and routine can drown or drain your sensuality and turn your WOW into a whimper. Lori Bryant-Woolridge's *The Power of WOW* helps you examine your preferences and habits, and offers refreshing, practical alternatives. The book will add ginger to your day with its upbeat tone and irreverent advice. It is self-help with flair. Read it and do it!"

—Dr. Linda Clever, Author of *The Fatigue Prescription*

"Many women experience an attrition of their 'WOW factor' simply due to the busyness of their daily lives. After long days of work, family obligations, socializing and all that makes for the life of a modern woman, how much WOW can you have left? Turns out, a LOT, with L⸺ �⸺ ⸺elage in her fantastic book. I recon⸺ ⸺ a must-read self-care manual for ⸺

—Nina Lesowitz, C⸺ *⸺ank You*

"Whether due to loss, divorce, breakup or those 'last ten pounds,' at some point in her life, every woman in the world feels like she's lost her mojo—her innate ability to not just appear sexy, but feel that way as well. Lori Bryant-Woolridge goes beyond the typical 'light a candle and put on some lingerie' approach to regaining sexiness and sensuality. She shows women how to find the sexy within, bring it back ... and keep it! Strap into your finest footwear, spend some time with Lori and get ready to meet the woman you are meant to be."

—Carole Brody Fleet, Award-winning author
of *Widows Wear Stilettos*

THE POWER OF
WOW

THE POWER OF
WOW

A GUIDE TO UNLEASHING
THE CONFIDENT, SEXY YOU

BY LORI BRYANT-WOOLRIDGE

viva
EDITIONS

Published in the United States by Viva Editions, an imprint of Cleis Press Inc., 2246 Sixth Street, Berkeley CA 94710.

Printed in the United States.
Cover design: Scott Idleman/Blink
Cover photograph: amana productions inc.
Text design: Frank Wiedemann
Shoe illustration: Samantha Hahn

First Edition.
10 9 8 7 6 5 4 3 2 1

Trade paper ISBN: 978-1-57344-656-3
E-book ISBN: 978-1-57344-677-8

Library of Congress Cataloging-in-Publication Data

Bryant-Woolridge, Lori.
 The power of WOW : a guide to unleashing the confident, sexy you : earn your masters in sensual arts at stiletto university / by Lori Bryant-Woolridge.
    p. cm.
 ISBN 978-1-57344-677-8 (pbk. : alk. paper)
 1. Sensuality. 2. Sexual attraction. 3. Women. I. Title.
 BF575.S42B79 2011
 646.70082--dc22
                                    2011011232

CONTENTS

DEDICATION

This book is dedicated to my lovely daughter, Eva Gabrielle, who is the true embodiment of sensuous beauty; and to Mother Nature, that divine goddess who makes everything she puts on look perfectly sexy and breathtakingly beautiful.

"Removing the veil from something that already exists is different from me trying to teach others the secret of how to live a better life."

—PAULO COELHO

ACKNOWLEDGMENTS

Have you ever had a dream that seems to take forever to materialize, but when it finally does, you know the timing is exactly right? Writing and publishing *The Power of WOW* is one such dream for me. This is the most important and personal book I've written to date, and I can't tell you how thrilled, grateful, and awed I am that it is finally in your hands.

You would not be reading this if not for the hard work and dedication of the amazing women who have enrolled in Stiletto U and helped tweak it and mold it into the effective set of lessons it has become. Their successes bolstered my confidence in the Stiletto University program as they proved that they were indeed becoming the confident, sensual women they wanted to be by using it. Thank you, ladies! I love you madly!

Thanks also to the publishers and staff of Viva Editions, particularly the lovely and talented Brenda Knight. Thank you for believing not only in my message, but in my ability to deliver it. Thank you, thank you, Sara Camilli. You are phenomenal and I am so happy and grateful to have you in my corner.

And last, I'd like to thank you for picking up this book and trusting me to help you unleash the incredible femme you are meant to be. Enjoy your journey, and please do stop, smell, and savor the flowers along the way!

Lori

INTRODUCTION: 9 WEEKS TO WOW

"I want to be less self-conscious and more comfortable in my own skin."

"After finding out about his affair, my self-esteem has been shattered. I want my sexy back, not for him, but for me."

"I wish I could be more aggressive when it comes to sex, but I don't want to seem loose."

"At forty-two, I want to truly enjoy sex with my mate."

"Between kids and work, I don't have the time or energy to be sexy."

"I want to feel sexy and confident in all aspects of my life, not just the bedroom."

"I seem to be projecting the wrong something, because I'm still manless."

"I'm tired of being alone."

Sound all too familiar? Kind of like the conversations you and your girlfriends have been having for years? Since you're reading this, I'm guessing you're feeling somewhat lacking in the sensuality/sex/romance departments of your life and you're looking for a remedy.

Well, happily, you're in the right place. And kudos to you for even picking up this book, because admitting to yourself that you're not on top of your game in the womanly wiles department takes courage. I'm mean, we're supposed to know all this stuff, right? How to be sensual and alluring and dynamite in and out of bed.

Like her.

You know who I'm talking about. Ms. Thing. You're sitting in a bar minding your own business, thinking you're looking cute and hoping someone else is going to think so too. And then here she comes. She sashays confidently into the room oblivious to the fact that all eyes, including yours, are on her. She's wearing the perfect little black dress (the one you've been searching for but always see on some other woman) and strutting over to the bar in a way that makes every body part sway with come-hither appeal. It's a walk that brings men to her side and sends women into private places to practice. You feel both jealousy and admiration toward this diva. Talk about paling by comparison. Suddenly, you don't feel so cute. And of course, she sits down right next to you and instead of ordering the cocktail du jour like every other girl in the room asks for some drink you've never heard of.

On closer inspection, you see that she's more striking than beautiful. More sensuous than sexy. Of course, within minutes, some Chris Rock-looking guy is elbowing you out of the way to get to her. You watch her handle the admirer, graciously accepting his compliments with a "you're-so-sweet-but-this-is-never-going-to-happen" smile and sending him back to his friends thinking he's Denzel Washington. You realize then that the key to her irresistible charm is confidence. This is a woman who is totally at ease with herself. A woman to study and emulate, not envy.

She has the power. That indefinable "wow" that seems to inhabit a lucky few and evade the rest of us. But you want it too. But where did she get it? And where do you start?

The truth is, most of us don't know what we're doing, and from the beginning our sex lives have been "Pretend until you win" propositions.

Think about it: Who taught you to be a healthy, sensual, confident sexual being? Who showed you how to feel good in your own body today, in the here and now, not tomorrow, when you've lost 10 pounds or the promises made by your cellulite cream are kept? If you're like the majority of American women, regardless of age, race, religion, or marital status, the answer is no one. And yet, do you know any woman who at one time or another didn't wish she was sexier? Or felt more confident in her ability to attract and entice a lover? Or had the courage to match her sensual thoughts with sexual actions?

Society has done a pretty good job teaching women how to be good at what we *do*. We're busy college students, power players with demanding careers and families, working or stay-at-home mothers with terrific (and demanding) tots. Department managers or soccer moms, we're trained to be super at our jobs. But forget the job, what about the woman?

See, nobody teaches us how to be good at who we *are*. In fact, rather than teach us, they seem to go out of their way to confuse us—particularly when it comes to the essence of our sensual, sexual selves. It's as if they said, "We'll give you all the education and training you need to be an amazing [fill in your job position], but when it comes to being an interesting, courageous, passionate woman, you're on your own."

The fact is that millions of women in this country, no matter how varied their wants and needs, are itching to get their sexy back. Not a month goes by when there isn't some magazine or Internet article or television segment focused on the topic of how to be more sexy and alluring. And the great majority of women (including nearly all the women I coach) seem to have a common desire: to shed their good-girl ways and add a little naughty to their nice.

It's true. Most of us were taught to be good girls. But even then, we were only told what good girls *don't* do, which made the list of what good girls *do* mighty short, and the list of things we were curious about and *wanted* to do extremely forbidding.

And so here you stand, wondering why your inner needs don't match your outer persona. Why your secret desires are in opposition to your cultural or religious upbringing. Why you're dying to change but have no idea where to begin.

Just where does one go to learn how to be a confident, lovely, and lusty *lady?*

Welcome to Stiletto U, a virtual university dedicated to teaching you how to unleash the confident, sensual you. Through our comprehensive, user-friendly, nine-week program focused on the power and pleasure of sensuous living, every woman can learn to be a healthy, sensual, charming, sexual being without the approval or validation of anyone other than herself.

Why Stiletto U? Because as a little girl, what's the first

thing you did to emulate a woman? Put your precious little feet into Mommy's high heels. High heels, particularly stilettos, have always been a metaphor for a woman's feminine power, sensuality, and sexuality.

But what if your chosen footwear is flats, and heels are reserved only for special occasions, if ever? Fear not, these lessons are for you too—it's the grown-up and sexy stiletto *mentality* that we're trying to impart. The idea that no matter your body shape, weight class, bra size, hair color, or heel height, you are always ready to walk tall, strut your stuff, and announce to the world that sexy has just entered the building!

You've gone long enough settling for living vicariously through the romantic escapades of Hollywood starlets and romance novel characters. It's time to make your fantasy life a reality. So just click those fabulous heels three times—and away we go to unearth and unleash the confident, sensual power of WOW in *you*.

Lori

WELCOME TO
STILETTO UNIVERSITY AND
THE POWER OF WOW

WELCOME!

I'm so thrilled that you've decided to join us! My sincere desire is to plant the seeds, and supply the tools necessary to help you blossom into the sexy, sensational, sensual woman you are meant to be.

I REALIZED THAT...
"SU is the best thing that has happened to me
in a decade. I just want you to know that this class
will make you a *woman*, not just put you in the position
to have more sex."
Dina '08

Stiletto U and *The Power of WOW* were born out of a lifetime of living sensually and encouraging others to do the same. In fact, this accumulated experience has resulted in my developing a career as a sensuality coach. After traveling around the country giving workshops and meeting women like you, women who are eager to get their WOW back (or claim it for the first time), I created and began teaching this curriculum through individual coaching, workshops, and adult school classes. I'm so pleased to tell you that the program really does work!

The women who graduate from Stiletto University are not the same women who sign up. They embrace the SU teachings and leave much more sensuous, definitely sexier, but most importantly, happier and more confident about *who* they are, exactly *as* they are. Let me share with you one comment from Maria, a Stiletto U graduate from Flint, Michigan. I think it really captures the Stiletto U experience: "I thought this program was going to be about flirting and outer techniques. I wasn't expecting to look at my inner self. I was surprised by how much I learned about myself. I have reconnected with the real me and it feels fabulous!"

You may find that it isn't always easy to look at yourself squarely as you begin to explore yourself from a different vantage point. My goal is not to create a *new* you, but rather to bring into balance your feminine side, the side that gets lost as you try to be everything to everyone else in your life—whether friends, family, or some mythical ideal that you've got in your head. At Stiletto University, we are in search of the true, sensual you. That may feel like a daunting task, but trust that the things you learn will show you not how to *play* the role of dynamic, sensual woman, but rather how to genuinely *be* that woman on your own terms, utilizing your exceptional gifts, talents, and looks.

So what makes *The Power of WOW* different from all the other books and programs on the market? Most tutorials on this subject treat sensuality as something one pulls out of her sexual trick bag, enforcing the erroneous idea that women should *feel* sensual only when they are *acting* sexual. But by eliminating sensuality from our daily lives, we too often find ourselves living without truly feeling *alive*. At Stiletto U, we believe that living daily through one's senses, or as I like to call them, the Fan Five (as in fantabulous!), is the bedrock of a pleasured and empowered life. Our program operates from the core idea that by initially separating your sensuality from your sexuality and teaching you to live a sensory life, pleasure becomes the norm, passions are discovered and ignited, and your confidence and WOW factor soar both inside and outside the bedroom.

Here's what SU alum Gigi from Naperville, Illinois, had to say: "This program is so much richer than its fun exterior would indicate. It's really centered around issues of authenticity and self-worth, and the benefits are there not for just the personal/intimate relationships, but for all relationships. Through Stiletto U, I woke up to appreciating and being more alive in the world, and that's a gift worth its weight in gold."

Like Gigi, you will learn that sensuality is an untapped power source that can have a profound effect on the way you view and interact with the world. You'll learn how to elevate your sensual-esteem and maximize your distinctive sensuality to create an extraordinary atmosphere in which to work, live, and love.

That's why, once you've earned your MSA (Master of the

Sensual Arts) degree, we do not bestow on you the title of Goddess or Diva or Sex Kitten or Bombshell or Bad Bitch. Our belief is that most women have spent their lifetimes trying to play a role, at the expense of their self-esteem and essential truth—and that living fully as themselves is natural and empowering and the ultimate sexy. As a Stiletto U student, you will simply graduate into a more whole and vital you—in your purest, sexiest, most authentic form.

So, again, welcome to Stiletto University. It's time for you to discover the delicious lost side of you that makes being a woman so much fun!

OUR MISSION

Our mission at Stiletto U is to unleash a woman's natural and individual sensuality, with the ultimate goal of making her feel comfortable and sexy in her own skin. We are dedicated to the idea that a truly sexy woman lives by her own truth, attitudes, and desires, and we strive to help her become the confident, sensual woman and partner she was born to be.

STILETTO U STUDENT BODY

Stiletto University students run the demographic gamut. Single, married, and divorced women of all ages and races, with or without children, can (and do) benefit from our program. While their lifestyles may be different, they all have in common the desire to tap into their inner strength, beauty, and feminine confidence.

YOUR PROFESSOR

Lori Bryant-Woolridge is an Emmy Award-winning writer and best-selling author, sensuality coach, and advocate for healthy, sensual lifestyles. She has authored three best-selling books, including *Weapons of Mass Seduction*, a sensuality manual within a novel, and has edited the erotic anthology *Can't Help the Way That I Feel*. Lori conducts sensuality classes and workshops around the nation, has been featured in local and national media including the *Seattle Times*, the *Detroit Free Press*, the *New York Daily News*, *Essence Magazine*, *Romantic Times*, *Working Mother Magazine*, *Cosmopolitan UK* and *Psychologies Magazine* (UK), and has appeared on numerous radio and television shows across the country.

MY SENSUAL JOURNEY

Okay, that's the official biography—but here's the one that really counts. Now in my fifties, I am wise and seasoned by age and life experience, and I fully live the life I promote. I am an active and productive flirt (my biggest charm achievement: I met my husband and became engaged in six days) and a lifelong sensualist.

It seems that most of my adult life I have been complimented for being sensual, charming, or sexy. And I don't mean to sound egotistical, because I'm definitely not. I'm doing what I ask all women to do, what I had to learn to do myself—listen to, learn from, and live the compliments I receive.

You see, like many of you, I may have had all those attributes, but I didn't always *own* them. Throughout my teens, twenties, and half of my thirties, I was doing what most of us do—the basic "fake it till you make it" strategy. And I was successful, both socially and professionally. I didn't know how or why, and frankly, it didn't matter, because whatever I was doing was working. But like a lot of women, after marriage and my first child, I lost myself. The role I'd been playing since I'd started dating had changed entirely. My body was different, as well as my mind-set. Suddenly, child care replaced self-care. I lost the me in Mommy, and my mind, body, and soul were in transformation. Was I a sexy mama or just my baby's mama? I wanted to be both, but how could I tend my maternal cocoon and still emerge a butterfly?

This is when my individual study and passion for understanding the sensual arts truly began. Every cocktail party conversation became a focus group, every flirtation an experiment in cause and effect. Life became my laboratory and I became my own case study. I began analyzing the successes and failures of my sensual approach to life by isolating my personal and flirting styles and test-marketing my ideas and techniques in my everyday existence. I have spent the past 20 years observing, researching, and breaking down my individual approach to living a sensual, charming, seductive life.

Here's what I learned: By putting sensuality at the core of my feminine existence, I became more aware, grateful, joyful, spontaneous, adventurous, and successful, both personally and professionally. (Oh, and you will notice that these are the same words you probably use when speaking of improving your *sex* life). The more I learned about and began to trust my version of "sexy woman," the more I began to accept and take possession of my ideas on love and lust. I learned that with true ownership of one's genuine self came pride in possession and the quiet demand for respect. I learned that the best technique for achieving success in all areas of my life (sex included) was to simply get to know myself and then happily *be* myself.

My confidence in my own power soared. People noticed. By request, I start giving informal "seminars" at my club meetings and girls' nights out. I wrote novels whose characters carried my sensual message. And then I penned *Weapons of Mass Seduction,* a sensuality manual within a novel. To promote the book, I began doing workshops instead of readings. Soon I was receiving speaking requests from organizations and conferences around the country. Readers' emails and audience comments confirmed that my ideas about sensuality and charm were helping women improve their personal lives; others asked for more direct advice. When the individual requests for extended help began to grow, my individual coaching career was born. I became a sensuality coach and have loved it from the very beginning.

What I have learned through living sensuously has carried me through the ups and downs of a long-term marriage and the identity challenges of many birthdays. Living sensually has expanded the passion and joy in my life because I have learned to revel in my physical and spiritual attributes and live by my own truth and convictions.

I proudly pass these lessons on to you—teacher to student, mentor to friend, woman to woman. While I've included bits and pieces from my personal journey, the bulk of this book is an extension of my individual sensuality coaching. I've tried to capture on paper the same sense of personal care and concern I give each of my students. I hope you feel the love—it is there, nestled between every word.

THE SU SEMESTER:
GAIN THE POWER OF WOW

The Stiletto U program is designed to help you establish your sensual mastery in three distinct units—**Individual WOW, Social WOW,** and **Sexual WOW.** Each unit contains an introduction, three classes and one living laboratory, and each lesson builds on the next. While the living lab is your opportunity to apply the lessons you've learned and solidify them in your lifestyle, everything you learn should be applied daily throughout the program.

Here is how it all works. Supplemental Philosophy of WOW readings are included in the laboratories and should ideally be done over the weekend to reinforce your unit lessons. Each lesson includes a brief lecture, class assignments, a note-taking (journaling) assignment, and a daily field trip—a 20- to 60-minute affirming walk (stilettos not required!). Class assignments cover everything from setting up your sensual sanctuary to infecting as many people as possible with your smile to allowing your "bad" girl to come out to play. If you devote a minimum of 90 minutes per day to your classwork, which can certainly be allocated throughout the day, you will be ready to unleash your sensual self onto the world in nine weeks. That's the ideal. But the program is designed for you to take as long as you need to learn and to live the Stiletto University mentality: *Being yourself can never be wrong.*

SUPPLIES AND MATERIALS

Along with this book, you will need a journal for your note-taking assignments and for recording any additional thoughts that come to you on your path toward sensuous living. Class assignments vary in their requirements for additional supplies. It's a good idea to skim ahead each week to see what you will need to complete your assignment. Most items can be found around your home, but you may end up buying new items to support and enhance your newfound sensuous lifestyle.

EARNING YOUR MASTER OF THE SENSUAL ARTS

If you're thinking, I don't have time for this, stop! The entire SU program is based on pleasure, self-acceptance, and finding joy where you stand. I have spent years testing and perfecting this curriculum through my workshops, classes, and individual coaching. It is designed to be user-friendly, practical, and flexible enough to accommodate your individual needs and schedules.

Spend one day or one week on each lesson. Stay on one class as long as you need and move forward when you feel ready. You choose the pace of your learning and sensual unleashing. Most of your assignments can be incorporated into preexisting areas of your everyday life. But it's important to do something *every* day, because fully enrolling yourself in Stiletto University obliges you to take time out for yourself each day to discover and explore the things that make you irreplaceable in this world. This is why you'll find a Student Contract to sign, pledging to love and appreciate the person who gets the least amount of your time and attention—you.

Here's what Dina (an SU alumni you'll meet at the

upcoming student mixer) said in her final exam: "My advice to those taking this course would be to look at it like real school, not some self-help book you can read in a couple of pages and put down. The same energy you put into learning English 101 you need to put into this course. Also, like any class, the effort you put in will determine the results you get at the end."

Ultimately, this is a journey of major realizations. At the end, you will find yourself saying, "I realized that ... ," and these nuggets of self-wisdom will be the foundation of your amazing new self. Look for these realizations from former SU students along the journey.

So, yes, earning your MSA will require work on your part, but I have to say, Stiletto U will be the most fun you ever had in school!

STILETTO UNIVERSITY STUDENT CONTRACT

I, _____ , agree to:

▸ Take action daily toward my sensual goals

▸ Be present and prepared for my class sessions

▸ Be honest about my challenges and what I want to achieve

▸ Be gentle and nonjudgmental toward myself and all new revelations

▸ Revel with joy and wonder in all my new discoveries about my sensual world and self

I commit to work on my sensual self for a minimum of nine weeks with the same love, dedication, and understanding that I give others in my life.

Signed _____ Date _____

STILETTO UNIVERSITY ENTRANCE EXAM

Please take a moment to answer these questions thoughtfully and truthfully. Your answers will form the basis of your Stiletto U experience and help you set your individual goals. At the end of the semester, you'll take a similar final exam to see how you and your views about your sensuality and sexuality have changed.

THE WOMAN:

1. List three words to describe your personality / physical appearance.

    a._____   a._____

    b._____   b._____

    c._____   c._____

2. On a scale of 1 to 10, rate your
   a. Self-esteem
   b. Feminine confidence
   c. Sexual confidence
   d. Social confidence

3. Name three women you admire, and tell why. What are your feelings about the impact they have on you? Do your feelings lean more toward inspiration or envy? Why?

a. _____

_____

_____

_____

b. _____

_____

_____

_____

c. _____

_____

_____

_____

4. To date, what has been your most defining moment (positive or negative) as a woman? How has this shaped your current perception of yourself?

_____

_____

_____

_____

5. What do you love most about being you? What do you most dislike?

_____

_____

_____

_____

6. Complete this sentence with the first word that comes to mind: I am _____

_____.

7. A person meeting me for the first time would initially notice my _____

_____.

8. What role does sensuality (defined as living through your five senses) play in your *everyday* life?

_____

_____

_____

_____

9. Recount your most sensual moment to date.

_____

_____

_____

_____

THE CHARMER:

10. List three words to describe a woman who flirts.

a. _____

b. _____

c. _____

Are your words mostly positive or negative? (circle one)

11. Complete this sentence: Personally, I think flirting is ____

_____.

12. I find it difficult / easy to converse with strangers. (circle one)

13. On a scale of 1 to 10, when it comes to being charming, I'd rate myself as a _____.

THE LOVER:

14. On a scale of 1 to 10, how would you rate your sex life? _____

15. Are you a sensual / sexual / or accommodating lover? Circle all that apply.

16. Complete this sentence: When it comes to sex, if I could change one thing about me, I would be _____

_____.

17. What keeps me from being more [insert answer from #16] _____

_____

is_____

_____.

18. My_____is the sexiest part of me.

19. What role does sensuality play in your *sex* life?

_____

_____

_____

_____

20. Think about the most rewarding / passionate / exciting sexual experience you've ever had in your life. State what made you feel that way about it and how you felt about yourself during this encounter.

_____

_____

_____

THE STUDENT:

21. Why did you decide to pick up this book and enroll in Stiletto University?

_____

_____

_____

_____

22. What do you most hope to achieve through this program?

_____

_____

_____

_____

23. Complete this sentence: You'll consider this experience a success if you _____

_____.

24. To complete your enrollment, register at www.stilettou. com.

STUDENT MIXER:
MEET THE STILETTO U ALUMNI

Before we begin this high-heeled journey together, I thought it might be a good idea for you to get to know some of the wonderful Stiletto University alumni[1] who will be popping in and out throughout the semester. These are just a few of the students who have utilized and helped tweak the Stiletto University program, and are now out in the world living their power of WOW.

They range in age from 25 to 52. Some are married, some divorced; others have never wed. They are mothers, stepmothers, childless. Some women have been with their husbands and lovers for years, others a few months. Some

---

1 While the essence of each student story is real, each is a composite of several SU participants with similar feelings and/or experiences. All names and identifying details have been changed to protect the privacy of the Stiletto University alumni.

incorporated their mates into their schoolwork, while others studied in private and let their lovers reap the rewards. A few are celibate, some by choice and the others by chance. And while some are rebounding from the pain and isolation of marital infidelity, others are coping with a multiseason man drought. One is taking back her life after an abusive sexual experience stripped her of all trust and sexual identity. Needless to say, they are an eclectic group, with different wants and needs, yet all are itching to get their WOW back or claim it for the very first time.

Some came to Stiletto U with hang-ups derived from a lifetime of trying to kowtow to the ideas of the Three P's (Parent, Preacher, Public Morality) of who they should be. All have hit at least one of the inevitable bumps along life's road—heartbreak, childbirth, middle age, divorce, infidelity—that caused them to stop and question their sexual prowess or relevancy.

Each is a victim to a culture and media that send divergent and ultimately harmful messages to women about what's sexy and attractive (read: young, thin and cosmetically enhanced).

They enrolled in Stiletto University with various levels of sensuality, and, like you, they came in search of a missing part of themselves—a part so deeply buried within that some couldn't even identify the problem. But they wanted a cure for the nagging sense of ennui, low self-esteem, low feminine confidence, or a lackluster love life.

All, I am happy to say, graduated with a greater understanding of their true selves and a richer sense of sensuality, empowerment, and feminine confidence. They still have ups and downs, but they are now better equipped to handle the hiccups with grace, flair, and a self-assured understanding that through it all, they remain magnificent.

So, without further ado, let me introduce several of our SU alumni. Mix and mingle among yourselves. No doubt you will see yourself in one or several of their stories.

POST-BABY SEXY
—SAY HELLO TO NATASHA

One is not born a woman. One becomes one.

—SIMONE DE BEAUVOIR

"I signed up for Stiletto U when my baby was eight months old because I was in need of some serious fluffing and fun."

On her entrance exam, Natasha described herself as funny, reflective, and a thinker. Physically she viewed herself as styleless, frumpy, and nondescript—a far cry from her single days, when she felt attractive and sensual. Before giving birth, Natasha felt comfortable socializing and considered herself a charmer. But not so much, post baby.

> **Natasha, Class of '07**
> Home: Connecticut
> Age: 32
> Married 4 years
> 8-month-old daughter
> **Personal Ratings** (1–10)
> Self-esteem: 7
> Feminine Confidence: 4
> Sexual Confidence: 4
> Social Confidence: 7
> **What Brought You to SU:**
> "Feeling rushed, anxious, and fat is not a sensual combo."

"Overall, I am a very sensuous woman, but since my daughter's birth, my feminine confidence feels low, like a 3 or 4 on a scale of 1 to 10. Sensuality and sex is almost nonexistent since we had the baby. We are always tired or overworked."

Natasha came to Stiletto U feeling like a lot of new moms: lost and trying to redefine her sexy. She was confused and angry about the changes in her body and her attitudes toward her disrupted sex life. Natasha was fighting hard to hold on to the sexy young woman she was before becoming a mother, disregarding the fact that her life, her body, and her relationship had changed forever. Our goal was twofold: 1) to help Natasha find her identity again as a wonderful lusty woman/mother, no matter what her new dress size was, and 2) reestablish a loving, fulfilling sex life based on her new family normal. Later we'll share the one powerful lesson that Natasha learned to help put her back on track.

ALUMNI TIP

"Sometimes the classwork felt like too much for a working mama with an infant. I did the walking field trip every day with the baby and each week picked one core assignment from each class and concentrated on that. The great thing is that you can go back and do the book more than once and have new learning experiences with the material you haven't done yet."

GOOD GIRLS CAN BE SEXY TOO
—MEET BRENN

Intellectual passion drives out sensuality.

—LEONARDO DA VINCI

"I never felt fulfilled in any of my romantic relationships. Not even my marriage. I was married for ten years to a man whom I was never physically attracted to because I believed that intellectual compatibility was the lifeblood of a good relationship, and that sex was my duty. We had sex, at best, twice per year. I've always seen sex as something bad, certainly not to be enjoyed and only done in the dark."

On her entrance exam, Brenn described herself as "easy to laugh but reserved, curvy, wears a size 10 shoe." Brenn also admitted to being cold and dismissive of any

> **Brenn, Class of '07**
> Home: Massachusetts
> Age: 38
> Divorced
> 14-year-old daughter
> **Personal Ratings** (1–10)
> Self-esteem: 10
> Feminine Confidence: 3
> Sexual Confidence: 2
> Social Confidence: 6 '
> **What Brought You to SU:** "I had the opportunity to spend the night with my 'fantasy' guy and couldn't even kiss him back. I just froze and was totally embarrassed. I realized that I'm not comfortable with my sexuality. I feel that a whole person is missing from my life."

admirers who approached her, because she was unable to accept their interest as genuine or honorable.

Brenn grew up in a very conservative household, under the watchful and extremely religious eye of her grandmother, whose desire for Brenn to be a "good" girl was so strong that she was stripped of any sense of her sensuality/sexuality. She was taught from her earliest years that only whorish women enjoyed sex, and that belief has haunted her throughout her life.

But it wasn't just her sorry sex life that was causing her angst. Brenn had also tied her sensuality so tightly to her sexuality that savoring life was unthinkable. She was afraid to allow herself to live sensually for fear that she would be "totally overwhelmed and become a loose woman." Even casually touching others or being touched troubled her, because in her mind, it came with sexual overtones.

"I was smiling all the time, but my life was miserable. I'd meet men and the more attracted I was to them, the more reserved and protective of myself I would become. Once they wanted to start a relationship, I couldn't deal. I would pick them apart until I decided that they were boring." Hiding behind polite distance and disingenuous laughter was Brenn's defense mechanism. She'd been trained to trust neither the intentions of men nor the compliments they gave her.

"I came to Stiletto U because I am intellectually sexy. I know that somewhere deep inside I am very sensual and I really want to live it. Yet I am struggling with the idea that if I do, that makes me a whore."

Brenn was like a lot of women who are confident and successful in the workplace but unable to find that same success in their personal lives. She was in desperate need to

connect—first with her sensual self, and then with her confident, assertive, sexual side that was not afraid to ask for what
she wanted in life or in bed. Hers was a tough and emotional
journey, and later you'll see how far she's come.

ALUMNI TIP

"The assignments are very effective and I did them
regularly. Sometimes I didn't go in order because I
wasn't feeling a particular subject, so I would move on
to another that I felt more emotionally connected to and
then go back later to finish the others."

SEXY BUT STILL ALONE
—SAY HELLO TO VIRGINIA

Men look at themselves in mirrors. Women look for themselves.

—ELISSA MELAMED

Virginia, divorced for 10 years, was ready and willing to get back in the relationship game, but despite feeling comfortably sensual and confident about herself and her femininity, she was still single and lonely. Self-described as strong, funny, beautiful, and voluptuous, Virginia was socially engaging and had no problem meeting men, but she rarely made it past two or three dates. Her relationship prior to joining Stiletto U did last for several months, but proved to be sexually unfulfilling and a confidence crusher.

> **Virginia, Class of '07**
> Home: New Jersey
> Age: 42
> Divorced
> **Personal Ratings (1–10)**
> Self-esteem: 8
> Feminine Confidence: 7
> Sexual Confidence: 6
> Social Confidence: 7
> **What Brought You to SU:**
> "I was tired of being alone but didn't know what I was doing wrong."

"I felt really confused because even though I felt comfortable flirting, when it came down to a relationship and actually having sex, it wasn't working."

When she enrolled in Stiletto U, Virginia had removed

herself from the dating scene. Her frustration level was high and climbing; while she was sure that she had what it took to attract and maintain a great relationship, she felt that the poor quality of the men she was meeting was holding her back. Virginia could feel herself shutting down socially, and that scared her.

"I just lost my zeal for being sexy and all that that entails. I wanted to be in a relationship, but had no idea how to attract what I was looking for, and I was tired of being disappointed by the men I was attracting.

"I came to Stiletto U because I seem to be projecting the wrong *something*, because I am still manless. At forty-two, I want a relationship where I can truly enjoy sex with my mate."

Virginia was looking for what we all seek: a loving, passionate relationship with someone we enjoy and who enjoys us. What she had forgotten was the universal rule "Energy attracts like energy." Our goal for Virginia was to help deconstruct and understand the kind of energy and the image she was presenting to the world, and then build up her true self and her ability to fully live her life without waiting for someone else to recognize and validate how wonderful she was. Later you'll see how changing her energy and attitude improved Virginia's quality of life.

ALUMNI TIP

"I loved the purposeful walks. They helped me to relax. On the way out, I really worked to stay in the moment and be in touch with my surroundings, and I used the way back to acknowledge the faults I have to work on, but embrace the positive that is me as well."

CHEATED OUT OF MY SEXY —HELLO, ANTOINETTE

Life consists not in holding good cards but in playing those you hold well.

—JOSH BILLINGS

At 52, Antoinette was living the "cougar" life with her 40-year-old husband. She was a doting stepmother to his three children, and while she still felt young at heart, she swore her mirror was telling her something different.

"My once tight body is now flabby and is not even attractive to me. I'm still as vibrant as a thirty-year-old, so it's even more discouraging to constantly be brought back to earth by my bedroom mirror."

> **Antoinette, Class of '08**
> Home: Florida
> Age: 52
> Married 8 years
> 3 children under 12
> **Personal Ratings (1–10)**
> Self-esteem: 6
> Feminine Confidence: 6
> Sexual Confidence: 4
> Social Confidence: 7
> **What Brought You to SU:**
> "I want my sexy back, not just for him, but most importantly, for me."

Like Natasha, Antoinette was a mom fighting to accept her changing body. Her husband's comments about her aging physique, and her own insecurities about getting older, had taken a real toll on her body image. But Antoinette had an even bigger problem.

"Two years ago, my husband confessed to cheating. I had viewed my marriage through rose-colored glasses, believing that nothing could penetrate it. Now, I view not only myself, but the world differently."

On her entrance exam, Antoinette described her appearance as "short and voluptuous," and her personality as "hesitant and modest." The self-doubt that came with her husband's infidelity only added to her physical and emotional insecurities.

"We were both caught up in the 'Let's do it and go to bed' routine, especially with both of us working and three active children. I no longer blame myself for his affair, but I know I changed after we got married. My focus shifted from being a good wife to being a good stepmother, and I admit that for a long time, I'd just been going through the motions of being a wife.

"He cheated with a woman I knew from work. This woman is the total opposite of me. She's more sexually adventurous than me. After I found out about the affair, I became extremely self-conscious about my body and sexual performance. I also was angry that it hadn't mattered to him what a good wife and mother I was. He had practically destroyed our family over *sex*."

Antoinette found herself in an odd predicament. Sex, the thing that was supposed to intimately bond her with her spouse, had become the thing that had driven them apart. "I became frigid and unforgiving, and very unsure of myself in bed," she said.

She'd become sexually frustrated and desperately wanted to break out of her good-mom mind-set and be a "bit more freaky." She was still physically attracted to her husband

and wanted to try to make their marriage work again, but wondered if she was still attractive to him. "I can't get past my thoughts that he's probably more focused on my love handles than on the experience."

Antoinette's goals for herself sorted into two distinct areas: 1) restoring her self-esteem so that she could stop seeing herself as a victim and start taking control of her life, and 2) boosting her feminine and sexual confidence so she could unearth her passions, be more assertive about her sexual needs, and enjoy sex with her husband again on her own terms.

Picking up the pieces of one's shattered life is no easy feat. At the next mixer, you'll see how Antoinette stopped looking for her husband to make her feel sexy and desirable and how she learned to seduce herself and reset the power balance in her relationship.

ALUMNI TIP

"There were some assignments that I asked other people to help with. I sent out an email to five men and five women with some of the note-taking questions and asked them what they thought about me. It was very telling and most helpful. I was surprised how much I learned about myself."

LYING TO BE SEXY—
MAY I INTRODUCE YOU TO DINA

*Beauty—when you look into a woman's eyes and
see what is in her heart.*

—NATE DIRCKS

Meet Dina, a 32-year-old wife, mother, and rebellious wallflower. As she readily admits, "I really didn't think that this was going to work for me. I thought I was deformed or something, that I was just meant to be the socially awkward one, the woman who didn't really have any femininity. I was resigned to being the matron."

When she enrolled in Stiletto U, Dina described herself as self-disparaging, bookish,

> **Dina, Class of '08**
> Home: Michigan
> Age: 35
> Married 7 years
> 4-year-old twins
> **Personal Ratings (1–10)**
> Self-esteem: 7
> Feminine Confidence: 4
> Sexual Confidence: 4
> Social Confidence: 7
> **What Brought You to SU:**
> "I hope to gain greater confidence in my womanhood and know what if finally feels like to be sexy, and to like sex."

and sporting the librarian look (complete with holiday-themed sweaters). Fearful of rejection, she was determined to make fun of herself before anyone else could. Highly intelligent, Dina used her smarts and humor to overcompensate for her lack of sensuality.

"Sensuality does not play much of a role in my everyday life. I try to wear clothes that aren't too tight; I usually eat while reading; I try not to get too musty by the end of the day."

Dina openly admired women who flirted and who saw flirting as "a great way to get free stuff." Despite her positive attitude on the subject, she was disappointed in her own charming abilities. "I can always make people laugh, but I feel like a clown, not a woman."

Married seven years to her college sweetheart, Dina found her marital love life at an all-time, ho-hum low. As she put it, "We have two boys, and both of us work full-time, me during the day and him at night. We don't have much of a sex life." And truth be told, what little they did have Dina wasn't enjoying.

Self-described as an accommodating lover, Dina was extremely insecure about her abilities as a lover and totally off-base about her husband's sexual expectations. She was also keeping a few secrets and needed to get them out in the open. "I have a decade of one big lie and several smaller lies to overcome. If I could change anything when it comes to sex, I would be more truthful about my needs. I am so grateful that I put the work into SU. I have changed from the core. This was a life-changing experience for me."

Dina was another hardworking Stiletto U student, and also one of several who incorporated her husband into her lessons and used him as a very willing laboratory partner. You'll see how putting the effort into finding her sensual self unleashed an entirely new woman and helped move her marriage in a more honest direction.

ALUMNI TIP

"I just want women to know that this book will make you a *woman*. The exams are more like surprises. You have to go out and use what you learn and see that it works, so it motivates you to keep going and really make the changes. I wish traditional schools would do this; then maybe I wouldn't have flunked Bio."

TOO SHY TO BE SEXY
—HEY, JANINE

Bloom where you are planted.

—PROVERB

Meet Janine, the baby of the bunch at 25. Single, with no children but with a brand-new boyfriend, Janine, self-described as painfully shy, quiet, and curvy, came to SU in an attempt to raise her self-esteem and feminine confidence.

Citing Josephine Baker as one of the women she truly admired because "she didn't care what the world thought of her, but did what made her happy," Janine signed up for Stiletto U hoping to learn how to do the same. "I want to feel sexy, confident, and sensual in all aspects of my life, not just the bedroom."

Still in her twenties, Janine lacked the life experience to understand and put into true perspective her limited sexual experiences. She was hurt by a domineering past lover and is now in a new relationship with a great guy, but she was

> **Janine, Class of '08**
> Home: Pennsylvania
> Age: 25
> Single
> **Personal Ratings (1–10)**
> Self-esteem: 6
> Feminine Confidence: 6
> Sexual Confidence: 6
> Social Confidence: 5
> **What Brought You to SU:**
> "I want to push myself out of my comfort zone so I can enjoy life more."

confused about how to walk the fine line between loving fearlessly and protecting her heart.

"In my last relationship, it felt as if I had to almost beg my ex for attention, time, and affection. It was very one-sided. When I left the relationship, I vowed that I'd never allow myself to be treated that way again. When I met Chris and we started talking, I was so caught up in not getting hurt again, that I just brushed off the things he said to me and kept my options open. I don't always allow him to lead in our relationship, because of my need to control everything in my life so that I don't get hurt again. He's never done anything to hurt or disrespect me, yet, at times, I put my guard up. I don't want to love like that."

And with only a few partners in her short adult life, Janine is still trying to sort out her role and abilities as a lover as well as wrestle loose her good-girl baggage. "A big part of me is still too scared and ashamed to let go completely. I want to be more adventurous and bold, and less concerned with other people's judgments."

Those people include other women and co-workers, people Janine's shell of shy mistrust kept her from getting acquainted with. "I don't really socialize or interact with people I don't know. Many people think I am stuck–up, because I hate talking to strangers, but I don't like opening myself to being judged in any way. I usually eat lunch in my office alone. I want to open up and meet new people." Her shyness also kept her from pursuing her passion—graphic arts. Opening up, Janine revealed that she was afraid to fail, so she didn't even try.

At the next mixer, you'll see how simply opening up her life to the world around her increased Janine's confidence and changed her personally, professionally, and sexually in ways she couldn't have imagined.

ALUMNI TIP

"I like the way it's organized. Starting off by working on yourself gives you a solid base. I would definitely suggest reading ahead so you know what's coming up and can adjust accordingly. For instance, I was able to do the mindful eating exercise at a work reception even though it wasn't on the assigned day. This helped me fit more things into my schedule."

WEIGHTING FOR SEXY
—THIS IS CATHY

Curve: The loveliest distance between two points.

—MAE WEST

When she enrolled in Stiletto U, Cathy, 46, was voluntarily celibate, childless, and had never been married. She described herself in three words: short, bold, and overpowering. And while she was not a traditional beauty, her body image (Cathy is plus size) was not the reason she decided to enroll.

Though Cathy admits that her sensuality was something she routinely neglected and put on the back burner, she wanted to

Cathy, Class of '09
Home: Georgia
Age: 46
Single
Personal Ratings (1–10)
Self-esteem: 6
Feminine Confidence: 2
Sexual Confidence: 2
Social Confidence: 6
What Brought You to SU:
"I'm a 46-year-old woman who lacks confidence in most if not all of my relationships. I'm the friend people depend on but don't call to hang out with."

explore it so she could better understand the attributes others said she had, but she could not see. However, after our first conversation, Cathy came to a slightly different reason for signing up.

"I wanted to participate because I don't know what womanliness is. I don't know it and can't embrace it because, in my mind, being feminine is extremely negative."

Cathy, like many of us, was lost in what I call "the lexis trap": letting the connotation of common words define and ensnare her. To Cathy, everything the rest of the world viewed as feminine—softness, overt sex appeal, coquettish charm, and so on—she didn't see in herself and viewed negatively. In Cathy's mind, being feminine meant "acting subservient, phony, and above all, weak."

While Cathy defined being a woman on her own terms, she discovered it to be more an act of defiance than an affirmation of her true individuality. She hid her feminine confidence behind a tough, no-nonsense face in an effort to protect herself from being rejected. She'd done the yo-yo dieting thing to no avail, greatly disliked her body, and without fully realizing it had developed an attitude that kept people from getting close to it or to her. By the time she enrolled in Stiletto U, it all had begun to take its toll.

"I'm tired. Emotionally and mentally."

After ending a two-year relationship, Cathy had been voluntarily celibate for over four years. "Honestly, I am not interested in sex right now. My desire is numbed to the point that it's no longer a craving."

Cathy had two goals for her semester. She wanted 1) to figure out and come to terms with her ideas on femininity and what it mean to be a woman; and 2) to learn the art of flirting, in hopes of improving her social life. I suggested that we add a third goal: becoming more comfortable with her body and her sexual self by exploring her sensual celibacy. Cathy wasn't so sure. As she put it, "What's the point?" Later you'll see what she learned, and you'll be surprised at how doing just one little thing on a regular basis changed Cathy's entire attitude and her view of life.

ALUMNI TIP

"Definitely take your note-taking seriously. Don't half-step, because you'll only be cheating yourself. After it's all over, set your journal aside for two or three months and then sit down with it and reflect over what you've learned. Evaluate what worked, and whatever didn't, go back through the assignments again."

WHEN SEXY HURTS
—SAY HELLO TO GIGI

We never know what strength and revelations might be on the other side of our fears.

—JACQUELYN SMALL

Gigi, Class of '09
Home: Illinois
Age: 43
Single
Personal Ratings (1–10)
Self-esteem: 4
Feminine Confidence: 0
Sexual Confidence: 0
Social Confidence: 5
What Brought You to SU:
I won it as a door prize. A lot in my life seems to be leading me to explore this previously taboo part of myself.

Now—last, but certainly not least—Gigi. Having won her enrollment as a door prize[2], Gigi decided to redeem it because she "felt called to have it." She says, "I hope to open a door that's always been closed to me and see where it leads."

Gigi, in my opinion, has come the farthest of all the Stiletto University students I've had the privilege of working with. She came to Stiletto U resentful, hurt, and angry with the world, and with every right to be. Sexually abused as a preteen, her trust in men and sense of sexual self was brutally stolen. Gigi spent her teen years

---

2 Gigi was accepted into SU only after assuring me that she was under the care of a certified and licensed therapist.

picking up weight and hiding her burgeoning womanhood behind it. When I met her at age 43, she had never had a relationship, intimate or not, was working an impossible work schedule, and was struggling to see her body, now nearly 150 pounds lighter, as a blessing rather than a curse.

"My weight always defined me, and without it, I haven't felt much definition at all, particularly as a woman, because I never felt like one before."

On her entrance exam, Gigi described herself as "average and rumpled, intense and guarded." Any attention paid to her previously invoked anger and resentment, and her interaction with men was driven by fear. Her social life, limited as it was, mainly revolved around her church activities. Gigi came to Stiletto U sick and tired of being mad at men and the world, but she had no idea how to change what she'd been feeling for her entire adult life.

Like Cathy (though for different reasons), Gigi was struggling to define what being a woman meant to her. And like Brenn, because she'd shut down her sexuality, she'd closed off her sensual side as well, cutting out much of the pleasure from her life.

"I don't take the time to enjoy things that I consider sensual—eating a good meal, a nightly bath ritual, putting on satin pajamas—unless I am really mindful about it, because I easily get trapped in my head."

Gigi also had mixed feelings about putting herself out into the world on a social level. While she described a woman who flirts as "bold, daring, and confident," she viewed the ability to charm and flirt as "overrated," and cited fear as the reason she was not more outgoing.

By keeping herself holed up and hiding inside big clothes

and an impossible workload, Gigi had achieved exactly what she wanted: isolation from any chance of being socially and sexually available. After our first two sessions together, Gigi was able to admit that her current lifestyle was lonely and boring, and she was interested, if not quite ready, to make a change.

Working together, we identified several goals for Gigi's semester: 1) to separate her sensuality from her unfortunately warped sense of sexuality so she could begin living life in Technicolor instead of the drab black-and-white version she was enduring; 2) to define and come to terms with what it means to be a woman and use her own definitions to boost her feminine esteem; and 3) to become more comfortable interacting on a social level, particularly around men.

Because of her past, Gigi was very resistant to any discussions about sex and sexuality. Much healing needed to take place before she was able to squarely look at herself as a sexual woman. At the next mixer, you'll see what she learned about her sensual self and sexual energy, and you'll be pleasantly surprised at how a simple compliment from a total stranger changed Gigi's life forever.

ALUMNI TIP

"Participate full-out and move through whatever excuses come up. I found the homework and the experiences of applying the lessons to the real world the most helpful. Even if I didn't do all of them, being mindful of the ones I did do, and showing up differently in the world, led to experiences from which I received either overt or covert feedback that was beneficial."

Stay tuned. You'll meet up with these alums and a few others in each semester unit and catch up on their progress so you can share their SU experiences and see what an impact living and loving sensuously has had on their lives.

INDIVIDUAL
WOW

CHAPTER ONE

SEN 101-INTRODUCTION TO SENSUALITY

THE PITY PARTY PROJECT

One of the assignments I often give my students prior to beginning the Stiletto U program is to take a mental health day from work or a weekend to throw yourself a pity party. I'm a big proponent of the occasional "whine and freeze" party because they are very liberating. They allow you to stop and honor your feelings of frustration, hurt, and anger so you can look them in the face, move past them, and continue forward. And while you might think it all sounds a tad lame and self-indulgent, think again. We often don't realize how comfortable we become, stuck in the mire of our negative emotions. Sure, these emotions are distressing, but in an awful lot of cases, anger, hurt, and fear become our comfort zone, merely because it's what we know. And for some of us, it's our guaranteed way to get attention—even if the attention is not healthy or growth inducing.

A pity party is a way to signal to your subconscious that it's time to move on. It's time to push away the darkness of your negative emotions and reactions and step into the light of positive feelings and mindful action. So set a date, and let's get this party started!

Once you have a date, the most important thing for you to do is to establish a time limit. One to three days of wallowing, as one student put it, "in the mud of misery," is plenty. As experience has shown, more than likely you'll be bored to death before your official end time and ready to shake off the self-pity and get on with self-improvement. So here are a few quick rules for your Feelin' Sorry Soiree:

▸ Set a start and end time. If you have responsibilities, make sure they're covered.

▸ No guests. Seriously, why subject anyone else to your misery?

▸ PJ's are the perfect attire to go with wads of Kleenex.

▸ Only fattening comfort foods allowed.

▸ Keep alcohol to a minimum. This is not a drunken binge. You need to be able to wallow and self-reflect, cry and curse the gods (but not the porcelain one), and ultimately clear your head and heart in preparation for the work ahead.

▸ As your issues surface, honor them. Don't shoo away the emotions they bring up; allow yourself to feel them. Bring your journal and record your feelings. The purpose of your pity party is not to try to figure it all out, but to purge so the healing can begin.

▸ Make a list of all the negative habits, people, and thoughts that bring you pain and you wish to purge from your life. Or perhaps you can write an honest and heartfelt letter to that person who has stolen your joy. Now make a list of all the positive habits, thoughts, and actions you want to manifest in the future.

▶ As a concluding activity at your Forlorn Fiesta, burn the negative list or letter (do not send that letter!), affirming to yourself that you are releasing all of what has been holding you back. Tuck the positive list somewhere safe, where you can periodically take a look and remind yourself of the woman you are becoming.

▶ When your Sad Social is over (or you're sufficiently bored), clean yourself up and commit yourself to recycling your *woe* into *wow!*

Okay, done with the sorry party themes! Now, turn the page to begin the process of unleashing the confident, sensual you.

JUST HOW SENSUAL ARE YOU?

When you hear the word *sensuality*, what is the very first thought that pops into your mind?

I'll pause while you ponder.

Okay, raise your hand if you said, "Sex."

If you did, it's okay. You're not wrong, just a little misguided. Most people do think that sexuality and sensuality are synonymous. We've been trained that way. And for sure, sensuality is a key ingredient in achieving a richer, more satisfying sexual experience. But sensuality is much more than a sexual perk. To be sensual means to be actively aware of your surroundings and find joy and pleasure through touch, sound, sight, taste, and smell.

Our five senses are as much a gift as our intellect and intuition, but along with our intuition, taking time to understand and enjoy them is often the first thing we eliminate in our quest to become intellectual, cultured, and productive human beings.

Here's a little pop quiz. Below, make a list of five gifts that you would give a friend at her baby shower and note the purpose of each item. (Ignore the basic necessities like diapers, bottles, car seat, etc.)

1._____

2._____

3._____

4._____

5._____

Now, looking over that list, I'll bet that most if not all of your gifts have something to do with the sensual pleasure of the impending arrival. (And if they didn't, make a note of that.)

Okay, I know you're asking, What does this have to do with making me sexy?

SHOEBOX WISDOM

The most effective kind of education is that a child should play among lovely things.

—PLATO

Here's my point: From birth to around age five or six, there is nothing we surround our little ones with that isn't designed and intended to stimulate every one of their senses with a variety of appealing tastes, sights, sounds, scents, and textures. From the very beginning, we wrap our children in a loving, sensual cocoon in an attempt to make their young lives pleasurable and happy.

And then, somewhere around six or seven, we rip away the cocoon and quickly turn our sensual butterflies into busy bees. This happens around the same time their lives become a series of scheduled events, just like ours, and time is of the essence. Nothing is done for sheer pleasure anymore; we must now accomplish something. There simply isn't time to stop to smell the flowers and flit and meander about. Our kids, just like us, have places to go, people to see, and play dates to attend. Long, playful tub time is replaced by quick bird baths and showers. High-chair food fests become car-seat meals in an effort to get to Gymboree on time. Music becomes a mere tool to pass the time or to beckon the Sandman. Visual stimulation now comes in the form of learning. Sensory delight is replaced by academic pursuit.

Around the same age, something else happens to strip our children of their God-given gift of sensuality. They discover self-pleasuring. We begin to associate their sensuality with sexuality and things change drastically. Suddenly, sensuality is discouraged and becomes adultlike, something we dust off when we want to spice up our sex lives.

Now ask yourself: Why is sensuality considered a birthright, an imperative in infancy and the toddler years, and then snatched away before puberty as if it is an unnecessary luxury? Living sensuously is what puts the delight in the mundane. It makes life interactive. What could be more necessary than that?

As adults in today's society, we basically purchase our sensual experiences, whether it be dinner on the town, a spa visit for a massage, or going on a Hawaiian or Caribbean vacation to feel the tropical wind on our face, see the magnificent sunset, or taste the salty lick of the sea. We ignore the beauty that surrounds us daily and, by doing so, become blind to its existence. But these days, so many of us don't have the disposable income to buy our sensual pleasures, and we're getting more and more disconnected from the full range of our senses and the everyday sense of contentment that is ours for the taking.

Thank goodness the fix is easy and free! There is so much joy buried beneath the everyday reality of our lives. Begin with nature. When you wake up to the world you feel engaged and energized in ways you haven't since you were a kid playing in puddles and finger-painting in the mud. By simply noticing the loveliness around you, you'll find that immediately you feel happier, and more connected to yourself and God.

Think about your lifestyle. Outside the bedroom, just how sensual are you? Do you save the soft sheets for company? Your favorite outfit for a special occasion? Do you buy flowers only for special events? Set the table and use the good china only when company is over? Light candles and put on sexy panties and perfume only when it's time to make love? Are you sensual only when other people are watching?

Sensual people relish the world around them, not simply observe it. They *experience* each task rather than rush through it just to get finished, and in so doing, live a more passionate and joyful existence, and still manage to get a heck of a lot done!

So it's time to take back your sensuality and revel in it once again. Savor life's pleasures. Pay close attention to the wonders of the moment. Focus on the sweetness of a ripe strawberry or the warmth of the sun on your naked arms. Stop looking at your sensuality as a sexual perk and start enjoying it 24/7. Because when you feel like a sensual woman, you behave like one. And that confidence is the true secret to owning the power of WOW!

EXAM

Just how sensual are you? Here's a quick test to help you determine how strong a role sensuality already plays in your life. There are no wrong or right answers. Knowing where you stand will help you know where you need to go.

1. The best part about wearing fur (real or faux) is:
a) How it feels.
b) Its warmth.
c) The attention it brings.

2. Given a free hour, you would:
a) Get a massage.
b) Listen to music.
c) Clean the house.

3. You accidentally wander onto a clothing-optional beach. You:
a) Strip down *au naturel* and join the party.
b) Lie out in your bathing suit and enjoy yourself.
c) Keep your head down and get the hell out of there.

4. You walk into a boutique and a violinist is playing. How does the music affect your mood?
a) You stop and let the music wash over you, absorbing all the emotion in the piece.
b) You stop to briefly enjoy the music and then resume your shopping.
c) You're totally focused. Your mood isn't affected at all.

5. Your choice of fruit would be:
a) A succulent mango.
b) Ripe strawberries.
c) A firm, ripe banana.

6. How often do you wear perfume?
a) Every day.
b) On special evenings or occasions.
c) Never.

7. You walk by a vase of gorgeous flowers. You:
a) Stop to inhale the floral scent.
b) Admire them as you pass.
c) What flowers?

8. What do you wear to bed?
a) Nothing but a smile.
b) Sexy silk or soft cotton nighties.
c) Sensible pajamas or T-shirt.

Add it up. How many: A's_____ B's_____ C's_____

Disclaimer: The purpose of all Stiletto University tests and exams is to provide fun and useful tools for thought and discussion. They are in no way scientific or diagnostic and are included for entertainment purposes only.

THE SENSUALITY FACTOR: YOUR SENSUAL STYLE

SUPERSENSUAL (Mostly A's): You are a pleasure-driven individual. You enjoy the thrill of living life through your five senses, which means that they are usually linked to your feelings. This makes you inclined to be emotionally passionate. Your lifestyle allows you to experience a life of maximum pleasure, but it's important to keep yourself in check, because the search for pleasure can be addictive. So to find happiness, seek balance. Too much of a good thing isn't always so good. But when properly directed, you have the innate ability to thoroughly enjoy everything life has to offer.

SOLIDLY SENSUAL (Mostly B's): You have found a balance between the practical and the pleasurable. You are able to enjoy and even lose yourself in the sensual aspects of life, but you aren't completely indulgent and know how to keep your emotions balanced. You are able to stay focused and to persevere, even while acknowledging the sensory pleasures around you. Continue to live in the moment and you will intensify your sensual side.

TOO SENSIBLE TO BE SENSUAL (Mostly C's): You are driven more toward intellectual or practical pursuits. You are tenacious, persistent, and goal-oriented. Like the supersensual, you need balance. You can expand your pleasure quotient by getting out of your head and exploring your world through your senses and by acknowledging how your body feels at any given time. You only have one life, so just make sure that you're not missing out on the sensual treasures of the moment by always trying to understand and analyze everything.

CHAPTER TWO

SW 102-SENSUAL WORLD
Lesson 1

It's time to revel in the world around you! In this unit on Individual WOW, you will begin the exciting process of getting back in touch with your sensual side by taking notice of and learning to savor this amazing world's glorious bounty through your five senses.

LECTURE: *Living sensuously.* To be sensual is to be actively aware of everything you see, smell, touch, hear, and taste. And when you live through the Fantabulous Five, you live in the moment. Why is this important, you ask? Because when you are in the moment, you are not worrying about the past or the future; your awareness of the beauty that surrounds you is intensified, which raises your level of appreciation and gratitude. (See how nicely this works? But wait, it gets better!)

PROFESSOR'S NOTES

Remember that the theme of each class assignment builds on the next. What you learn today should be applied tomorrow and every day!

It's a good idea to look over the lessons coming up so you can prepare ahead of time.

This new appreciation ultimately causes an attitude change and mood shift from frustration and dissatisfaction to happiness and pleasure. This has a *huge* bearing on how you perceive life, love, and, yes, sex. And in this positive, happier state of mind, you can begin to work your passions and enjoy all the magic that life has to offer. So make a commitment to yourself to take some time each day to notice and partake in the sensuality of the world around you.

TODAY'S SENSE: *Smell.* Our sense of smell adds richness to life in ways that we aren't always conscious of until it's taken away, and the quality of our life dramatically changes. In addition to being directly connected to taste, smell can instantaneously trigger vivid memories, strong emotions, and lustful attraction. From food smells to body odor, studies have found that certain smells turn men and women on and can help improve intimacy and sex. Smells also have the uncanny power to alter mood, and can make you feel calmer, sexier, or more confident. Yes, the nose definitely knows!

PROFESSOR'S NOTES

Note-taking or journaling is a major part of the SU program. Taking the time to record your delights and doubts will help you sort out the attitudes and ideas that you need to keep and build upon, and those you need to toss because they are holding you back.

Do a little sniffing around your world today. Find a scent in your home that you enjoy (soaps, lotions, shampoo, spices, food, potpourri). Take a few minutes to relax and enjoy a *scent*uous moment. Begin to isolate those scents that speak to your positive emotions, and begin to integrate them into your daily life. FYI: To clear your nose so it's at its smelling best, take a deep sniff of ground coffee.

DAILY FIELD TRIP: Today you will take the first of your daily 20- to 60-minute walks. Be present during this sensual journey and be witness to all the glory Mother Nature has bestowed upon you. As you walk, really notice the sights, sounds, smells, and textures around you. Be mindful of your thoughts while walking, but also try to stay aware and in the moment.

TODAY'S WALKING THOUGHT: *I am Mother Nature's grateful heiress.*

CLASS ASSIGNMENT: Spend today recognizing all the great and wonderful things you have inherited today. Make a pact with yourself to be fully conscious of every terrific thing that you receive for the next 24 hours. Think small.

Think grand. Smiles, sunshine, blue skies, rainbows, parking spaces, your house, your job, your family and friends. For every item you can count in dismay for not receiving, I guarantee there are five soul-filling gifts that you did inherit.

NOTE-TAKING: In your journal, record today's impressions of the world around you and your emotional connection to them. Note what most caught your attention on your walk. Which of your senses was most stimulated?

What did you learn about your sense of smell? Think about the smells you associate with loved ones, favorite foods, holidays, or your favorite vacation spot. Associate any memories you have with each of these scents. What memories, emotions, or physical changes did it trigger for you? If someone was asked to describe you by your scent, what would they say you smelled like?

I REALIZED THAT...

"I was so humbled when it came to all the material things we own. This week put things into perspective ... just be grateful."
Wanda '08

Make a list of all the things you have inherited today. For which are you most grateful?

EXERCISE: Begin with three sets of 10 kegels, three times a day. You can do them anywhere at any time. In the bed, shower, car, at the checkout in the supermarket.

Kegels are exercises to strengthen the muscles, called PC muscles, that support your pelvic cavity. They are the same muscles that stop the flow of urine when you void. They are also the muscles that, when in shape, help give you rip-roarin' orgasms!

If you have never done one before, they are simple to learn. Start when you have to urinate. Sit on the toilet, and as your urine begins to flow, try squeezing your PC muscles to stop it. Hold for 10 seconds and then release. Start and stop three times. If the urine stops, you're doing it right! If you can't stop it completely, don't worry. The PC muscles respond quickly to consistent exercise.

Lesson 2

LECTURE: *Everyday sensuality.* Adding sensual enjoyment to your chores brings beauty to the everyday details of your life, and doing so does not require that you add one more thing to your task list. With the right state of mind, you can make anything a sensual experience—eating, walking, dancing, gardening, housework, laundry. You name it, and there is a way to savor and enjoy it! So simple and yet so satisfying!

PROFESSOR'S NOTES

Here's a fun extra credit assignment you can do with or without your kids and fit in anytime you find yourself outdoors: cloud watching. Look up and find shapes in the clouds. Notice the blue sky and white fluffy clouds, see the sunbeams as they filter through angels' wings. Feel your stress begin to dissipate with the wonder of it all.

As you run errands, notice the sounds, sights, smells, textures, and tastes around you. Do your housework in pretty underwear and listen to music that rocks you from the inside out. Make dinner, even if it's just a salad, a sensual extravaganza. From the laundry room to the bedroom and everywhere in between, explore the sensual you and learn how to use your distinct sensibilities to create an extraordinary atmosphere in which to live, love, and of course, make love.

TODAY'S SENSE: *Sight.* Sight is the sense we depend on most to understand the world. We use our eyes in almost every activity we perform, whether reading, working, watching television, sending an email, driving a car, or gazing at our loved ones. But way too often, we're so busy *looking* that we don't truly *see* what is in front of us. Look up, look down, and all around. Pay attention to what catches your eye today and notice how those sights affect your mood. What glories surround you that you've been missing?

During the day, choose a familiar object or person to study. Look closely for details that you may not have consciously noticed before. Are there many? Are you surprised by your observations?

PROFESSOR'S NOTES

If you've really tried but your schedule doesn't permit you to make your daily field trip a separate event, incorporate your mindfulness whenever you are on your feet and moving. It may be your walk to the car or bus stop, or down the office corridor. The most important thing is to be fully present on the journey.

DAILY FIELD TRIP: Today you will take another 20- to 60-minute walk. Travel a different route to excite your senses, paying particular attention to what you see. Keep in touch with the internal sensations you experience as you move. Take each step with positive, appreciative thoughts.

TODAY'S WALKING THOUGHT: *I am Mother Nature's grateful heiress.*

CLASS ASSIGNMENT: Choose at least one task from your to-do list today and turn it into a sensual experience. For example: doing your laundry. Instead of simply stuffing clothes into the washer and then into the dryer and getting to the next chore, here's how to make it a sensual experience.

As you sort clothes, let your hands experience the different textures of the various fabrics. Notice the artwork you create with piles of color. Hear the whooshing of the wash cycle and notice how the sound vibrates through your body. What thoughts does that sound bring to mind? What experience does the scent of your detergent or fabric softener conjure up? Bring the warm towels from the dryer to your face and breathe in the scent before giving your cheek a soft caress, and feel the sensation of the soft terry nap as you fold it. You have added probably two minutes to your laundry time and yet suddenly it is an experience, not simply a chore.

I REALIZED THAT...
"This really helped keep my spirits up. Instead of letting my mind wander into all kinds of negative thoughts about my problems, it kept me focused on something pleasant."
Antoinette '08

The same sensual effort can be applied to doing the dishes, cooking, carpooling, gardening, bathing yourself and the kids, and so on.

NOTE-TAKING: In your journal, record your impressions of your task after making it a sensual experience. Include any emotional connections to these impressions. Note what most surprised you about this new perspective toward housework. Which of your senses was most stimulated?

What was the most interesting thing you saw today? What, if any, impact did this have on you or your day?

EXERCISE: Continue with three sets of 10 kegels, three times a day. Repeat your walking thought as you kegel.

VOCABULARY WORDS

Turn abstract words into concrete action. Write down the first word or phrase that pops into your head when you hear the words below. (Don't overthink it. This exercise will help give you a truer indication of how you feel about yourself.)

Curiosity: _____

_____

_____

Adventure: _____

_____

_____

Passion: _____

_____

_____

Imagination: _____

_____

_____

Gratitude: _____

_____

_____

Playfulness: _____

_____

_____

Joy: _____

_____

_____

Now go further and write a line or two more fully defining your personal thoughts about each of these elements. Then look up the actual meaning. How do your thoughts differ from the definitions?

On a scale of 1 to 10 (1 being lowest, 10 highest), rate how much these elements play a part in your life. In what ways can you apply them more diligently to your daily life?

Lesson 3

LECTURE: *Sensual sanctuary.* We all need a place of our own to relax and dream. And even with very little space, you can put together an area to honor yourself and your sensuality. Create a sacred space to think and journal and let your ideas and desires act out their dramas. The key is to remember that when you dwell in this zone, you are entering a special state of mind that will help you focus your energy on the project at hand—unearthing the sensual you.

PROFESSOR'S NOTES

There is a big difference between thinking only of yourself and taking care of yourself. Make time to nurture yourself and quit using "busy" as an excuse for not putting yourself on today's to-do list.

TODAY'S SENSE: *Touch.* Touch is our oldest and most pervasive sense. It's the first sense we experience in the womb and the last one we lose before death. And our amazing skin, which has about 50 touch receptors for every square centimeter (we're talking 5 million sensory cells overall), loves to be touched. This makes our skin a *huge* pleasure center. The thrill of touch comes not only through skin-to-skin contact, but through contact with all types of stimulating textures. We don't generally think of touch as a basic need, like hunger, but when we are without it, we slowly become depressed and withdrawn. With just one touch, we can communicate the depth of our feelings; we can nurture or destroy. The pleasure and power of touch is undeniable.

Wear something today that gives you pleasure to touch. From showering to having sex, make touch the foremost sense of the day, dwelling in both the physical sensations and emotional feelings it unearths.

DAILY FIELD TRIP: Continue your daily 20- to 60-minute walks. Find something—a flower petal, feather, leaf, stick—to carry and touch while you walk. See what you can learn new about this item through your sense of touch.

SHOEBOX WISDOM
Sensual pleasures are like soap bubbles,
sparkling and effervescent.

—JOHN H. AUGHEY

TODAY'S WALKING THOUGHT: *I am Mother Nature's grateful heiress.*

CLASS ASSIGNMENT: Turn a place—a corner, a table, your closet or dressing table, any area you can call your own—into a sensual sanctuary. It doesn't have to be elaborate, just personal and inspiring. Set up your sanctuary somewhere you will see it often, but make sure the space is private enough that you will feel comfortable leaving it up when company comes over. On top of a dresser or any other surface in your bedroom is a good idea, but if that is too public, you can set it up in your closet or bathroom. Include something from each of the five senses—personal things that remind you to feel sexy and sensual. Here's what's on mine: a green tea-scented candle; a hummingbird ornament; an inspirational affirmation; a peacock feather; a small bowl of smooth, black stones; a tin of tangerine candies; a smiling sun ornament; and my journal. Other suggestions for your sanctuary: a mirror, a photo, a table fountain, flowers, chocolate, a beautiful scarf or fabric, pearls or worry beads.

If you absolutely have no space to spare, put your items in a special box or basket and set up a mobile sanctuary at a kitchen or coffee table.

ASSIGNMENT #2: After you shower or before you go to bed, put on some soothing music and spend at least five minutes spreading a great-smelling oil or lotion all over your body. Don't hurry through this. Slowly cover every inch of skin and record the physical, mental, and emotional sensations you experience. Feel free to fantasize!

NOTE-TAKING: Sit in your sanctuary for at least 10 minutes and reflect on the items you've chosen. In your journal, write about what this collection of items says about who you are at this moment in your sensual life.

Write about how you feel about being physically touched and touching others. Think about your wardrobe. What fabrics do you like next to your skin? What sense do you dress for—touch or sight?

> **I REALIZED THAT...**
> "I had never really felt the fabric on my skin
> before. I will never buy clothes again without thinking
> about how they feel against my body."
> LaShawn '09

Are you the touchy-feely type? If not, why not? How often are you "in touch" with the people you love? How much time do you spend touching yourself?

EXERCISE: Continue with three sets of 10 kegels, three times a day. If you're forgetting to do them, try doing them each time you go to the bathroom, when you are in the shower, or when you are on the way home from work.

Lesson 4

LECTURE: *Mindful eating.* Mindful eating has the power to transform a simple bite into a blast of pleasure with every morsel that passes your lips. Sadly, most of us are caught up in the web of *mindless* eating—munching on countless meals that we barely taste, let alone savor. Food is one of the most sensual and satisfying pleasures we have, but most of us are too busy dieting or rushing through our schedules to truly enjoy eating. We have become a hurry-up society more concerned with calorie counts and fat content than appetizing dining experiences. We have traded the pleasure of eating for convenience and nutrition.

PROFESSOR'S NOTES

Mindful eating is not only going to make your meals markedly more pleasurable, but it's an excellent dieting tool because it lends itself to portion control.

It's also a very sexy way to eat your food, but more on that later …

By all means, eat healthily and watch your portion sizes, but don't shy away from the sensual satisfaction of food. To go beyond simply eating to truly tasting your food requires bringing your Fan Five to every meal. At mealtime, from your table setting to your menu, engage each one your senses—and find delight in the nourishment of your body.

TODAY'S SENSE: *Taste.* Taste helps us, among other things, satisfy our hunger and explore our world by choosing food we enjoy. The mouth, too, is a pleasure center, physically and emotionally, because food and emotions are tightly interwoven into the fabric our lives. There is a reason we describe certain dishes as comfort foods. Our associations with food and taste are as much about friends and family and special events in our lives as they are about eating. Many foods become our favorites because of the memories we have tied to them. And believe it or not, taste is one of the primary senses that will lead you to discover your only-one-of-its-kind individuality. Our taste buds recognize four categories of flavor—sweet, sour, salty, and bitter. These categories are often used to describe people. Are you a salty lover? A hot and spicy girl, a sweet or sour sister? How do your taste buds describe *you?*

Treat yourself to a new taste sensation with a food you're already familiar with. If you love Red Delicious, try a Granny Smith apple today. Milk chocolate lover? Go for dark. Wake up your tongue with new tastes and textures.

DAILY FIELD TRIP: Today, on your 20- to 60-minute walk, pick one of your vocabulary words (curiosity, adventure, passion, imagination, gratitude, playfulness, joy) to be the theme of your walk. Let your route and thoughts combine to actualize this theme.

TODAY'S WALKING THOUGHT: *I am Mother Nature's grateful heiress.*

SHOEBOX WISDOM

Nothing would be more tiresome than eating and drinking if God had not made them a pleasure as well as a necessity.

—VOLTAIRE

CLASS ASSIGNMENT: Enjoy a meal of several of your favorite foods. Take a bite of one dish, close your eyes, and before chewing, simply savor the taste, textures, temperature, and sensations created in your mouth. Now chew slowly, taking the time to savor every bite. Repeat with another dish. Make a note of the different taste sensations provided by different food groups. By comparing and contrasting, you can develop a keener sense of taste, which will enhance your enjoyment of food and might even make you a better cook!

NOTE-TAKING: In your journal, consider your taste preferences and how they influence not only your food choices but your moods and actions as well. Is there a correlation between your personality and your palate? What was your most savory, sensual experience with food? Write about it.

Next, devise a menu for a delectable meal to serve to yourself or your friends and family. Treat this as if it were an important family occasion, because what meal isn't more delicious when it's shared with people you love?

PROJECT: From the food shopping to the cooking, make the preparation for this meal a sensory experience and cook and serve when schedules permit. Make each dish tasty, with assorted textures and flavors. Serve the meal in a visually pleasing setting. Slow dinner down and take time to taste and enjoy every bite.

Make notes in your journal about how this experience of mindful eating has affected you and your time spent with friends and family. Record in your journal ideas, recipes, and other ways you can make mealtime more sensuous on a daily basis.

PROFESSOR'S NOTES

If cooking isn't your thing, order in or go out, but make your tasty class project a sensory excursion.

Another option would be to make this a potluck affair. Invite friends to bring their favorite dishes and indulge yourselves in a sensual tasting.

EXERCISE: Continue with three sets of 10 kegels, three times a day. Repeat your walking thought as you kegel.

Lesson 5

LECTURE: This class, Sensual World, is all about "coming to your senses." So what have we learned? That to fully experience the sensory and sensual thrills surrounding you, you need to pause, be aware, and be open to perpetual surprises. That to feel truly alive, you must nurture the sensations of awe and wonder and get in the deliberate habit of allowing sensory delight into your daily life. We've also learned that when you remain fully present in the *now*, painful past memories or upsetting future worries cannot disrupt your present happiness. As you take time to fully incorporate these lessons into your sensual world, know that you are a true heiress and the beneficiary of all that is beautiful and special in this world.

PROFESSOR'S NOTES

SW 102 is coming to an end. I hope you have managed to begin the process of unearthing your natural sensuality and now have new appreciation for the amazing world around you.

TODAY'S SENSE: *Hearing.* Each day, waves of sound wash over us and fill our world with constant noise. So much so that we filter out much of the hubbub around us. But without even realizing it, we also filter out the sounds that enrich our lives, whether music or the cheerful chirping of birds or the soft breath of our loved one sleeping beside us. How much do you notice and enjoy the lovely sounds around you? How much auditory bliss have you eliminated from your day? Are you hearing but not really listening?

Be actively aware of the sounds around you today and how different sounds affect you emotionally. Fill your day with the pleasurable sounds of laughter, music, nature, and the voices of the people you love.

DAILY FIELD TRIP: Today, walk with the intention of actively listening to the world around you and enjoying the symphony of sound that creates the soundtrack to your day.

TODAY'S WALKING THOUGHT: *I am Mother Nature's grateful heiress.*

I REALIZED THAT...
"This [program] has given me permission to simply enjoy. Wow! It's intoxicating. The shift is amazing!"
Rebecca '09

CLASS ASSIGNMENT: Spend at least 15–30 minutes in your sensual sanctuary or elsewhere listening or moving to music that you particularly enjoy. Now put on a new genre of music that is unfamiliar to your ears. If you usually listen to R & B, listen to Classical. If New Age ordinarily floats your boat, check out some Country. If you typically enjoy music with lyrics, make it a point to listen to jazz or a song sung in a foreign language, so that the vocals become another instrument. Or try some of nature's music and feast your ears on the sound of thunderclaps, ocean waves, or whale songs. Close your eyes and hear the music with not just your ears but your body and soul as well. Let yourself go—feel the way your body responds to the various instruments and sounds. Witness any alteration in your moods.

NOTE-TAKING: In your journal record your feelings about your musical interlude. Record your bodily responses and then your emotional ones. What did you learn about yourself through the music? Did you find certain kinds of music moved you more than others?

Think about your sensory exploration this week. Was one sense more represented than the others? If so, which one? Take a few minutes to explore that particular sense and what part it plays in your joyful pursuit of daily life.

Record your thoughts and feelings about what you learned about yourself this week through your sensual world and living sensuously. Do you notice a shift in your mood? Are you feeling lighter and a bit happier?

EXERCISE: Continue with three sets of 10 kegels, three times a day. Repeat your walking thought as you kegel.

Extra Credit:

SENSUAL WORLD MOVIE SUGGESTIONS

Want to see the concept of living sensuously in action? Check out one or both of the following movies. These are movies that flex your sensory muscles. They entice each of the Fan Five (yeah, even smell!) to the point that you almost feel you are experiencing the action. And even without overt love scenes, they all are *very* sexy. These suggestions beautifully illustrate the lessons you've been learning this week about your sensual world. Go fix yourself a yummy, tongue-tingling snack and watch, enjoy, and learn!

WOMAN ON TOP. Penelope Cruz plays a heartbroken chef who leaves her unfaithful husband in Brazil and heads to San Francisco, where she becomes the hit of her own sensual cooking show. This movie makes cooking seem so sexy even you microwave chefs might be tempted to break out the pots and pans!

A WALK IN THE CLOUDS. This is a sweet romantic story about a WWII soldier who falls in love with the daughter of a wealthy Mexican aristocrat in California. It is one of the most sensually packed movies I've ever seen. The scene where they are fanning the smoke from the vineyard—OMG!!

I love it, and I never seem to tire of its rich, luscious sensuality.

Watch. Learn. Enjoy!

Give yourself a grade based on the amount of work you did this week and how well you applied the lessons learned.

SW 102 CLASS GRADE:

_____

CHAPTER THREE

SY 103–SENSUAL YOU
Lesson 1

Welcome to Sensual You! While you will continue to discover and revel in your sensuous world, this class is designed to help you begin to *re*discover (or perhaps discover for the first time) the sensual enchantress within you that time, life, and other people's opinions have effectively buried. We begin by teaching you how to START and STOP your way to a new sensual you.

LECTURE: *Individual sensuality.* Most of us, in our heart of hearts, simply want to be noticed in this world. Some of us put a lot more effort into it than others, but for the most part, people want to be recognized. Generally, for women, this starts as a desperate need during puberty and carries on well into our adult years. Think about it: How much time, effort, and money have you put into hairstyles, cosmetics, and fashion trends in order to stand out in the crowd, only to find that everyone in the crowd looks basically the same? (Think of the overstyled celebrity award shows where individuality has been erased from glamour.) Or only to find that you still don't feel comfortable with your appearance? Kind of defeats the purpose, don't you think? Or have you done the opposite and created a personal style and persona that forces people to notice you, but for all the wrong reasons? Either way, you're playing a role and dressing in a costume.

PROFESSOR'S NOTES

Your Fan Five will give you clues to your individual tastes that set you apart from others. The fact is, a woman's sensuality truly takes root in her individuality. A woman comfortable in her uniqueness is a confident woman, and a confident woman is a sexy woman!

One of the most amazing benefits of living through your Fan Five is that you can't help but begin to understand yourself better. Your special sensory preferences become clues to who you are at your truest level. And it's from this true you that you begin to build a personal pizzazz that is neither a put-on nor a duplicate of anyone else's.

The power of true you: Now we're talking WOW!

SENSUAL YOU RULE #1: STOP trying to change yourself to fit an image and START changing your self-image.

Trying to force yourself into someone else's idea of who you are and what you should look like is setting yourself up for a heapin' helpin' of frustration and rejection. But changing the way you look at yourself obliges others to do the same—on your terms.

SHOEBOX WISDOM
Beauty is how you feel inside and it reflects in your eyes. It's not something physical.

—SOPHIA LOREN

DAILY FIELD TRIP: Today you will take your 20- to 60-minute walk with thoughtful emphasis on *you*. While you continue to enjoy this as a sensory experience, I want you to turn your thoughts inward, concentrating on your walking thought for the week.

TODAY'S WALKING THOUGHT: *I am.* Short and sweet and powerful, this is an important affirmation. It will help you integrate the idea that your value is in your very existence and that you are perfect as is.

CLASS ASSIGNMENT: *Creative visualization.* See yourself as you already are. Escape to your sanctuary for at least 10 minutes. Get in a comfortable position, whether sitting or lying down, where you won't be disturbed. Relax your body completely. Breathe deeply and slowly from your belly, release all tension, and let it flow from your body.

PROFESSOR'S NOTES

Creative visualization is the technique of using your mind and imagination to create the life you want. Many of you have been using it for years to manifest your negative thoughts without realizing it. How many times have you thought that you were unattractive or unlovable?

CV creates positive energy, which, like negative energy, will become reality. Also, by ending the exercise with the mantra, *This, or something better*, you are leaving room for something better than you ever imagined.

Check out the book *Creative Visualization* by Shakti Gawain for more information.

When you feel deeply relaxed, start to imagine the woman you want to be. If you want to be more confident in your body or sexually liberated or socially charming, imagine yourself in such a situation and see everything happening just as you want it to. If you want a good partner in your life, create that positive interaction in your visualization. You can imagine what you and other people are wearing, saying and doing, plus any details that make it more real to you. Have fun with this. It should be a thoroughly enjoyable experience, like a child daydreaming about what she wants for her birthday.

Now, keeping this image still in your mind, make positive, affirmative statements to yourself (aloud or silently, your preference). "I now have a sexy, loving relationship with myself." "I am a sexually evolved woman." "I love the confident, sexy woman I am." "I am in a happy and healthy relationship."

And as personal growth guru Shakti Gawain encourages, always end your visualization with the following: "This, or something better, now manifests for me in totally harmonious ways, for the good of all concerned."

NOTE-TAKING: Jot down in your journal how you feel about what you are manifesting.

EXERCISE: Continue with three sets of 10 kegels, three times a day. Repeat your walking thought as you kegel.

THE LEXIS TRAP EXAM

Have common words and their definitions ensnared you in boundaries set by someone else? Is your sensuality and feminine confidence caught up in the trap of connotation? Take a minute to jot down the first word or phrase that comes to mind for each of the words below. As with last week's vocabulary test, don't overthink this. Just write down the first word that pops into your head. Feel free to add any other words that restrict you from living life on your own terms.

It's true: Words have power. But you have control.

Sexy: *aluring*

Flirtatious: *Charisma*

Scandalous:

_____

_____

_____

_____

Lust:

_____

_____

_____

_____

Good girl: *inexperienced*

_____

_____

_____

_____

Bad girl: *loose*

_____

_____

_____

_____

Go further and write a line or two more fully defining your personal thoughts about each word. Then look up the actual definition. How do your thoughts differ from the definitions? Do you find that most of these words hold a negative meaning for you? If so, where do you think those feelings came from? Explore this in your journal.

Now give each of these words a positive connotation based on your personal moral code and sense of integrity.

Lesson 2

LECTURE: *See yourself through others.* She may be someone you have an innocent girl crush on, or someone you refer to as the "biatch" on days when you are feeling less than charitable. Or she might just be a stranger you notice in passing and can't keep your eyes off. Whoever they may be, begin to pay attention to the attributes of WOW in other women that capture your attention and awe. It's important to understand that the attributes you admire (and maybe envy) and are drawn to in other women are most often the same hidden assets that you possess but have yet to acknowledge and let surface. So look, listen, and learn from the women around you.

PROFESSOR'S NOTES

Funny how you will readily overlook the perceived flaws of those you love as unimportant, and concentrate on their other wonderful qualities, while you refuse to do the same for yourself.

Maybe not so funny, huh?

SENSUAL YOU RULE #2: STOP concentrating on what you don't have or don't like about yourself, and START embracing what you do.

Like every woman, you have at least one (if not two or three) physical features that you, for the life of you, don't see as special. It could be your eyes, your legs, your shoulders, your hands and feet. Whatever it is, enhance your assets and stop worrying about the rest.

DAILY FIELD TRIP: Continue with your daily 20- to 60-minute walks. Add a word to your walking thought today that most expresses the woman you are but haven't shown to the world. (I am ... fearless. I am ... seductive. I am ... beautiful.) Walk with that mantra in your mind and on your lips.

TODAY'S WALKING THOUGHT: *I am ...*

CLASS ASSIGNMENT: Today's assignment is to begin to listen to, accept, and learn from the compliments you receive. So many of us are too modest or insecure to even accept compliments, let alone see them and use them for the useful and empowering nuggets of inspiration they are. How many times have you brushed off a kind comment or made some self-deprecating remark in response to a compliment? Stop downplaying the wonderfulness of you! Give yourself permission to bask in the warmth of your own sunshine and be open enough to allow others to do the same.

PROFESSOR'S NOTES

How often do you compliment others? Are you generous in your recognition of the specialness of others? If not, maybe that's why you can't see the specialness in yourself.

A woman with WOW knows how to graciously take compliments for what they are, gifts from the universe, and use them to fuel her confidence—not her ego. If enough people tell you your legs are great or you have amazing eyes, you have a pretty good idea what about you is most special. People will also clue you in as to what colors look good on you or what styles really flatter your body. Once you are clear about your best features, own them and showcase them with pride.

NOTE-TAKING: In your journal, make a list of all the compliments people give you. Think about how you've felt when you've heard these things about yourself. Did you believe them, or question people's motives? Now add some of your own to the list of other people's compliments. Make a list of the things you admire about yourself.

EXERCISE: Continue with three sets of 10 kegels, three times a day. Repeat your walking thought as you kegel.

Lesson 3

LECTURE: *Define yourself through your own eyes.* Take time to truly admire yourself with loving eyes. Most of us don't really look at ourselves and our bodies, and when we do, it's usually only to critique them. That's why we don't learn to love and find beauty in them as they are. Spend some time with the lady in the looking glass. You'll be amazed at how fabulous she really is if you take the time to truly see her.

I REALIZED THAT...
"I came in with this attitude that, yeah, it's easy to feel beautiful and sexy when you already look that way. Now I know that it's easier to feel those things if you believe them about yourself. I've finally stopped comparing myself to other women."
Lucy '08

Why is this important? Because when you are comfortable and confident with who you are—mind, body, and soul—you no longer seek validation from others and instead validate yourself on your own terms and by your own standards. When this happens, nobody can shake your confidence to the point of paralysis. And once your realize that only you can let someone else steal your joy, the chances that you will allow them to do so will be reduced dramatically.

SENSUAL YOU RULE #3: STOP giving other people the power to validate you. START validating yourself.

Other people's opinions will always matter, but they should never be your guiding principle, more important than your own opinion.

DAILY FIELD TRIP: On your 20- to 60-minute walk today, add a second word to yesterday's walking thought. (I am ... fearless and sexy.) Step lively, girl!

TODAY'S WALKING THOUGHT: *I am ... ( ) and ( ).*

CLASS ASSIGNMENT: *Mirror, Mirror.* You'll need a full-length mirror and your journal. Arrange for 15–20 minutes of private time in your sensual sanctuary or bathroom. Look in the mirror and write down the first thoughts or words that come to mind when you look at your face. Make a list of three things you dislike about your face, and three you love. Now look at your naked body in the mirror and repeat the exercise, focusing on what you like and dislike about your entire body. Identify your one or two best features. Now turn the page and give yourself a heartfelt compliment.

M. lines
lines
over bite

hair
lips
eyebrows

skin color
breast
legs

fatty thighs
st. waist

NOTE-TAKING: In your journal, write about how difficult it is (or is not) to witness yourself naked. Is it uncomfortable to see yourself sans clothing? Why or why not? Next, write down and finish this thought: If my body looked exactly how I've always dreamed, my life would change in these ways ...

Now ponder this: What's easier? For you to be naked physically, or emotionally? To bare your butt or to bare your feelings? Why?

EXERCISE: Continue with three sets of 10 kegels, three times a day. Repeat your walking thought as you kegel.

Lesson 4

LECTURE: *Charisma*. It's the backbone of the WOW factor. Every woman has her own distinctive brand of star quality, and you don't have to be famous to flaunt and use it to your best advantage. Charisma is not *what* you are—your image or physical stature—but *who* you are, rooted in your personality. It's your own "secret sauce" that helps you connect emotionally, intellectually, and even spiritually to others.

SHOEBOX WISDOM

Check out your Fantabulous Five and see what clues your sensory preferences provide to help isolate your personal variety of killer charm.

Your personality charisma may be flashy or flamboyant. Maybe it's quiet and intoxicating, or warm and witty. It's probably a combination of two or more qualities, with one the most prominent and the most powerful display of your unique brand of WOW. Once you identify yours and comfortably claim it, it can never be taken away, nor will it sag or drag or disappear with age. It becomes the anchor of your sensual persona.

SENSUAL YOU RULE #4: STOP minimizing your successes and accomplishments and START acknowledging that you are a walking wonder.

DAILY FIELD TRIP: Today, on your 20- to 60-minute walk, wear those sexy panties that you've been saving for a special occasion and get out and strut your stuff.

TODAY'S WALKING THOUGHT: *I am … ( ) and ( ).*

CLASS ASSIGNMENT: Have you ever wondered why Michelle Obama, Sandra Bullock, and Jennifer Lopez are all considered beautiful and sexy even though they are so completely different? It's because they each understand their own personality strength—smart, funny, sexy—and work it to its maximum effect.

Study the following charisma types (on page 55) and select the group you think is most closely aligned with your personality. You may be a mix of charismas—we all are—but don't project the charisma you *want* to be, chose the dominant charisma you *are*. This way, just as with your best features, you're always leading with your strengths.

NOTE-TAKING: In your journal, consider some women you know who would share your type of charisma. How do they reveal their personality? What mannerisms, style of dress, tone, and so on, do they project? Now reflect on your charismatic style. Is there another style you feel naturally applies? Is there a charisma you secretly covet? Why? Do you currently recognize some of those charismatic traits in yourself?

How do you reveal your distinct charisma? Do you hide your true personality type under another? If so, why? If not, what can you do to further emphasize your charisma? Does your appearance match your personality?

EXERCISE: Continue with three sets of 10 kegels, three times a day. Repeat your walking thought while kegeling.

THE WOW FACTOR: YOUR CHARISMATIC STYLE

COOL CHARISMA:
Nicole Kidman, Salma Hayek, Halle Berry

Mystery is what makes a woman with Cool Charisma so appealing. She's classy and self-contained, and part of her allure is that you never quite know what she's thinking. Cool but never cold, she is ultratempting because her demeanor implies that there is much more to know and uncover.

SHOEBOX WISDOM
[Charisma is] about a sparkle in people that money can't buy. It's an invisible energy with visible effects.

—MARIANNE WILLIAMSON

CUTE CHARISMA:
Katie Couric, Jennifer Hudson, Reese Witherspoon

A woman with Cute Charisma is friendly and optimistic. She makes people feel comfortable around her and her appeal lies in the fact that she's approachable and inclusive. She may appear vulnerable and in need of protection, but this cutie is completely capable of taking care of herself.

SEXY CHARISMA:
Angelina Jolie, Jennifer Lopez, Tina Turner

Sex appeal and passion ooze from every pore of a woman with Sexy Charisma. Her sexuality permeates everything she does and yet she's no bimbo. Her soft, sensuous exterior belies her inner toughness, which makes her enormously enticing.

SMART CHARISMA:
Michelle Obama, Lisa Ling, Diane Sawyer

For a woman with Smart Charisma, her shining intelligence is her greatest appeal. And while she won't dumb it down for anyone, she's no intellectual snob. She has the unassuming ability to make you consider things in an entirely different light, which is her charming way of getting what she wants.

PROFESSOR'S NOTES

Remember that most personalities are a mix of charismas. While one is usually the most dominant, they are not mutually exclusive. A woman with sexy charisma can certainly be smart, and usually is. Cute can be powerful, humorous, mysterious as well. Bottom line: whatever the mix, it's all sexy as hell!

AMUSING CHARISMA:
Ellen DeGeneres, Whoopi Goldberg, Sandra Bullock
A woman with Amusing Charisma will attract you with her sharp wit and humorous take on life, all the while making you laugh and feel at ease. There's nothing clownlike about this kind of charisma. It's clever and disarming and draws you in like a magnet.

POWER CHARISMA:
Madonna, Oprah Winfrey, Hillary Clinton
A woman with Power Charisma has the audacity to go for her goals and yet remain deeply feminine. She is independent and fearless. Standing next to her, you might feel a little intimidated by her energy and intensity, but you're also fascinated.

Lesson 5

LECTURE: *Sensual signatures.* It's time to begin to cultivate your distinct sensual persona. A woman's sensuality truly takes root in her individuality. It's the little, very personal things that make you feel sensually exceptional and become the lingering clues to your inimitable personality. And because you aren't trying to be like everyone else, you will eventually find comfort and confidence in simply being yourself. So start acquiring the five signatures that every woman with WOW should have and make them part of your daily existence. These are not items found on the "What's hot" or trend lists of the season, but rather carefully considered finds that define you. Know that, initially, these signatures will serve as physical prompts to remind you who you are, but in time, they will become the things that you are known for.

PROFESSOR'S NOTES

I once interviewed the famed fashion stylist Lloyd Boston, who told me that women worry too much about looking fabulous all the time. "Understand that you don't have to look amazing every day. Save amazing looks for when it matters."

Well said!

Another great tip from the Style Guy: "Look at celebrities in reverse. Take notice of their worst fashion moments, determine why it doesn't work, and apply those lessons to yourself."

Check out Lloyd's book *The Style Checklist: The Ultimate Wardrobe Essentials for You.*

SENSUAL YOU RULE #5: STOP thinking you *want* to be sexy and instead START realizing that you *are* the new sexy.

Sexy is not a body type or a fashion style. Sexy is an attitude that starts in your head. Where it ends is what makes your body (and your lover) smile.

DAILY FIELD TRIP: Today, walk with the intention of strutting your stuff proudly.

TODAY'S WALKING THOUGHT: *I am ... the new sexy.*

CLASS ASSIGNMENT: *Shopping list.* Begin to identify your individual signatures and make a shopping list. Let's be clear. These are not elements of yourself that you put away in your closet and pull out for special occasions. These are the signatures that you build your brand of sensual WOW around, the features that make you stand out in the crowd and mark you as a woman who knows and likes herself. You're not trying to dress up and play at being a sensual woman—you are owning your unique sensuality and therefore simply being irresistibly you.

You can read more about branding yourself through your signature style in the Philosophy of WOW readings.

1. SIGNATURE SCENT. Express your *scent*uality. Choosing the scent you like enough to be your signature fragrance can be difficult because there are so many to choose from. If you haven't got it figured out yet, visit your nearest Sephora store. They have a simple touch-screen program to help you identify your signature scent based on your individual personality and style.

2. SIGNATURE SYMBOL. Identify your trademark icon, something that connects you to your sensual self and is a reminder of the ultimate woman you are striving to become. Identify a particular shape, word, or symbol you've always been drawn to and claim it as your own. Whatever your icon, recognize the positive emotions it evokes in you, define its importance to you, and let those feelings influence your behavior and the way you see yourself.

3. SIGNATURE STYLE. Sophisticated or bohemian, tailored or feminine, from your lipstick to your signature cocktail, develop a personal style and dress to express and impress yourself. Make sure that a large percentage of your clothing tastefully showcases your best assets. Identify your "uniform"—your go-to pieces you can put on without a lot of thought—for days when you are feeling less than stellar. Your uniform basics should have a flattering fit, be easy to wear, and be amenable to bumping up a fashion notch by adding a few signature accessories. Above all, they should make you feel stylish and attractive.

4. SIGNATURE SEXIES. What's under your skirt? Is what's under there in sync with what's going on in your head and your attitude about yourself? Whatever your style preference, just make sure your signature sexies are your brand of sexy and make you feel I've-got-a-secret terrific no matter what is covering them up. Your bra and panties should be clean and in good repair, matching or coordinated by color, supportive and well fitting. On a practical level, great-fitting undergarments also make you look better in your clothes. To get uplifted and lose the panty lines, start by going to a local lingerie store or department store that does professional fittings. Once you know the size, style, and brand that works for you, look online for deals and steals.

5. SIGNATURE SONG. What's your femme fight song? The one that makes you stand taller, smile broader, reminds you of the amazing female you are and brings out the sexy in you? Listen to it while you're driving, walking, or exercising. Use it to pump yourself up before a big date or event. Use your theme song to inspire your attitude and lift your spirits when your confidence levels sag.

PROFESSOR'S NOTES

Some signature songs to consider:

Just Fine (Mary J. Blige)

I'm Every Woman (Whitney Houston)

Golden (Jill Scott)

Whatever Lola Wants (Sarah Vaughan)

The Art of Seduction (Maxi Priest)

Feeling Good (Nina Simone)

Girl From Ipanema (Astrid Gilberto)

Sexy Back (Justin Timberlake)

Smooth (Santana with Rob Thomas)

Fergalicious (Fergie)

I'm Beautiful (Bette Midler)

Just the Way You Are (Bruno Mars)

Miss Independent (Kelly Clarkson)

All the Woman (Tina Turner)

New Attitude (Patti LaBelle)

Single (Natasha Bedingfield)

You Gotta Be (Des'ree)

Firework (Katy Perry)

NOTE-TAKING: In your journal, take a minute to identify what signatures you already own or recognize as your own. Write down what they mean to you and what they express about you. What did you learn this week about your individual sense of sensuality? Is the signature style you currently have showcasing the authentic you?

EXERCISE: Continue with three sets of 10 kegels, three times a day.

Extra Credit

TIPS TO GET STARTED ON YOUR SIGNATURE STYLE

1. KNOW YOUR BODY AS IT IS, NOT AS YOU WISH IT WERE. Not as you imagine it being, and not how you intend it to be in the future. Understand your best attributes (those great eyes or sexy shoulders or slamming legs)—those are the features you're going to dress to highlight. Just as important, know your body type and *perceived* imperfections. Every woman's got them, whether it's cellulite, jiggly arms, a minuscule bust, or saddlebag thighs. I say *perceived* because if your body met the current beauty standards, you'd look like a naked 12-year-old boy, and what's so damn perfect about that? We're women. We're supposed to be voluptuous and pillowy or toned and muscled and lean or (fill in your body type). Healthy and happy is the new beauty standard!

2. NEXT, FIND SOME QUIET TIME AND SIT DOWN WITH A STACK OF FASHION MAGAZINES AND STORE CATALOGUES. Unless your signature style leans toward the fashionista, avoid *Vogue* and all the high-fashion tomes—the more you can look at real women in real clothes, the better. Tear out all the outfits that catch your eye. You'll find there is a certain look or combination of looks that continually appeals to you. Now define that style for yourself in your own words. Is your preferred look regal and tailored? Maybe funky but elegant. Feminine and sweet? Earthy and bohemian? Are you drawn to bold color or muted tones? Do you like classic looks or trendy pieces? Discover the look you like and then head out to the stores and begin pulling together similar looks in styles that flatter and highlight your positives and camouflage your negatives.

3. FIND ACCESSORIES THAT ARE DISTINCTIVE AND SAY YOU. This includes jewelry, shoes, and lipstick. And don't be afraid to wear them in ways other than intended. Wear a necklace as a belt (or vice versa), or attach a funky pin to your handbag or shoes to create a one-of-a-kind look. Let the designer in you come out to play. Accessories are a cost-effective way to turn your basic uniform into an artistic expression of self. And be willing to extend this individualism to your social style. Why be just another woman sitting at a bar sipping a pink cocktail? Scour the bartender books and find a drink that becomes your distinctive version of "the usual."

4. EVERY WOMAN SHOULD OWN AT LEAST ONE PAIR OF CFM[3] SHOES. Nothing can make you and your legs look sexier than a great pair of heels. For decades, high heels have been recognized as the ultimate in sexy footwear. And with good reason: the height of the heel alters the wearer's center of balance, creating a walk that makes the hips sway and the bottom protrude; the style of the shoe makes legs appear longer and leaner; that same shape also arches the foot sexily. High heels make the wearer look taller and slimmer, creating an air of confidence and sophistication which is, in itself, sexy. And here's the cherry on top: Italian

---

3 (Come Fuck Me)

PROFESSOR'S NOTES

Most major department stores have complimentary personal shopping services. You can learn a lot about fit and fabric from them. Use one of these services, or a sales associate or a friend, to help you pull together your signature style. And even if you can only afford to buy one piece, make it a uniform staple and then get on with the fun of building high/low wardrobe around it.

Lingerie Online
Figleaves.com
Myla.com
Freshpair.com
Barenecessities.com

urologist Dr. Maria Cerruto, of the University of Verona, has concluded that walking in higher heels—and they don't have to be stilettos—gives a workout to the pelvic floor muscles, the pleasure muscles that are linked to orgasm. If you can't maneuver in stilettos, find a great, sexy pair of kitten heels in which to walk that golden gait. And remember, if heels aren't for you, let the cut and style of your shoe scream "I'm sexy" for you.

SHOEBOX WISDOM
"Look to the heel ... The sex is in the heel."

—LOLA FROM *KINKY BOOTS*

Give yourself a grade based on the amount of work you did this week and how well you applied the lessons learned.

SY 103 CLASS GRADE:

_____

CHAPTER FOUR

SLL 104-SENSUOUS LIVING LABORATORY

This week you will put the lessons of the last two weeks into practice and solidify your newfound sense of individual sensuality.

LECTURE: *So much to do, so little time.* Feeling just a tad overwhelmed? The trick is to find ways to incorporate sensuality in your daily life, not see it as another thing to add to an already overloaded schedule. Even if you can start with just one thing a day, it's still progress.

> ## I REALIZED THAT...
> "SU didn't require any more time.
> It just meant utilizing what time I was already using
> in a different way."
> Gigi '09

SENSUAL YOU RULES: Continue to apply one rule from the previous lessons each day this week, concentrating on the rule that most resonates with you.

SENSES: Did you notice which of your Fan Five was most dominant? This week, make a point of living through another one of your senses.

CLASS ASSIGNMENT: Meet God, joy, and yourself where you are, not where you want to be. Catch up on any assignments you didn't get to or would like to repeat from the last two weeks. Begin the search for your sensual signatures.

NOTE-TAKING: Take time to record your thoughts and feelings about what you learned about yourself through your sensual world and individual sensuality lessons.

EXERCISE: Continue with three sets of 10 kegels, three times a day.

The Philosophy of WOW

THE PERFECTION OF IMPERFECTION

Despite millions of steadfast believers, the mythical goddess named Perfection, just like Santa Claus, the Easter Bunny, and the Tooth Fairy, exists only in our imagination. In fact, far from being a goddess, the bitch is a green-eyed monster who has wreaked havoc on the minds of men and women, for ages.

The time, energy, and money we spend blindly pursuing an ideal that is not only unattainable, but in the end *boring* as hell, is mind boggling. I mean, really. If God had intended us to all look and behave the same way, do you think he would have hard wired self-expression, free will, and individual sensory experiences into our personalities?

The images we pursue are man-made and unrealistic, created to fool and entice us into the pursuit of retail happiness. By constantly stressing what is physically impossible to achieve naturally, businesses make us so insecure about our appearance that we're willing to contribute $160 billion a year to the global beauty industry. In the U.S. alone, we spend over $12 billion a year for cosmetic surgery, $24 billion on skin care products, $14 billion on makeup, and over $30 billion on weight loss products. And after all those billions, we're still no closer to that ideal of perfection.

In a *New York Times* article on celebrity endorsements, Eli Portnoy, a branding specialist, made the following statement: "The reality is, people want a piece of something they can't be. They live vicariously through the products and services that those celebrities are tied to. Years from now, our descendents may look at us and say, 'God, these were the most gullible people who ever lived.'"

It's time to end living vicariously through other people and live your own life. So instead of changing your nose or your bust size or even your wrinkle cream, how about changing your view? Stop looking in the mirror and start gazing out the window. Because when it comes to defining your sensual self, you need only to take a peek outside to see how it's done.

Mother Nature is one sexy weapon of mass seduction. She's the true embodiment of the power of WOW, the first and most authentic diva sex symbol. She's a woman who loves her incomparable attributes with no excuses and little compromise. She understands the perfection of imperfection. She recognizes the true beauty in individuality and the fact that one woman's mole is another woman's beauty mark.

SHOEBOX WISDOM
Confidence is Mother Nature's push-up bra.

—LORI BRYANT-WOOLRIDGE

Forget pinning your dreams on the celebrity set. Watch and learn. Let Mother Nature be your ultimate mentor.

Does the desert whine about the meadows getting all the flowers? Does she endlessly complain about her barren landscape or dusty tumbleweeds? No. She says, "Love my sandy, cactus-strewn behind as it is because I'm *hot*." She makes no apologies for her seemingly colorless terrain, but insists instead, "Find my beauty within or keep wasting your time trying to find that unattainable, perfect oasis. It's a mirage, you know."

Does the snowy femme make excuses for being cold and icy? No. She falls like snow, with gentle humility, and grins as you turn breathless with the exquisite hush of her bounty. Some player haters may call her frigid, but they're often the first to slide down her slopes or find themselves lying spread-eagled on her glistening white bosom, gleefully making snow angels. Yeah, she's one cool number, but you can't help being in awe of the individuality of each of her flakes.

And does the rose whine, "I'd be a beautiful blossom if I didn't have all these damn thorns?" No, she makes no excuses and knows you love her despite her bumpy stem, because you can't keep your nose out of her gorgeous buds.

Take your cue from Mother Nature. Love your natural self in all your natural beauty. Make no excuses for your *perceived* imperfections. Become comfortable in your own skin—big butt, little boobs, cellulite, whatever. The reality is that you're much more aware of your imperfections than those looking at you, and ultimately, you fret about them much more than anyone else—especially your lover.

Stop dwelling on your so-called flaws and begin to emphasize your best features—we all have two or three—with your inimitable style. Carry yourself with confidence and then dare the world not to find you, thorns and all, absolutely *fabulous*!

BRAND YOURSELF WITH
YOUR SIGNATURE SENSUALITY

Most truly distinctive women take great pride in their individual sensuality and personal brand of WOW. They have, through trial and error and dedicated effort, honed a look and an air about them that is personal and memorable. It's the little things they do or say or wear that make them stand out in a crowd. And because they aren't trying to be like everyone else, being themselves can never be wrong.

SHOEBOX WISDOM
For one to be irreplaceable, one must
always be different.

—COCO CHANEL

So how do you cultivate your own sensual signature style? At Stiletto University we start with a list of five sensual signatures that, every woman should own and make part of her everyday existence.

1. Signature scent
2. Signature symbol
3. Signature style
4. Signature sexies
5. Signature song

Every woman should have a *signature scent*. Finding a perfume you love and wearing it regularly (*regularly* being the key word) is an important step toward creating a memorable, sensual style. For you, it's a quick way to lift your spirits and arouse your sensuality and confidence, while for the people who get near you, it's a gentle indication of who you are; and for those who are interested, it's a lingering memory of a woman they can't forget.

SHOEBOX WISDOM

It [perfume] must be personal and lingering, not to be forgotten tomorrow. I want mine to say, "I have passed by, but here I still am."

—COCO CHANEL

I generally wear two fragrances, depending on where I'm going and what mood I'm in. For daytime and casual wear, I spritz on my current favorite, L'Eau par Kenzo. It's light and sexy and makes me feel flirty and playful. When I'm going formal or on occasions when I want to feel elegant and sophisticated, I wear Chanel No. 19. It makes me feel sensual and mysterious. I can feel my persona change when I have it on.

Notice I say that each fragrance makes me feel a particular way. Even though fragrance is mostly about your sense of smell, all your senses work together to inform your emotional state. And fragrance definitely has an effect on your mood and behavior.

Along with an unforgettable *scent*uality, you should have

your own *signature symbol* or trademark icon. Companies brand their image with logos so consumers can pick them out in a crowd, so why shouldn't you?

What exactly is a signature symbol? Think Mariah Carey's butterfly. It is something you can see and touch that connects you with your sensual, true self, reminds you of the woman you are striving to be, and gives the rest of the world a hint of who you are. Lots of power packed into such a little thing.

Where do you find your signature symbol?

What I suggest is to try to identify a particular shape, color, animal, flower, or motif that you have always been drawn to. Maybe it's a shoe or an orchid or a circle. Are you drawn to the moon, the ocean, a cloud, or an open eye? For me, it was the sun, mainly with faces.

For years, without really realizing it, I've been attracted to and collecting images of the sun on everything from vases to beach towels. When I designed my first business card, I unconsciously picked out a sun image as the logo. One day I was flipping through a book on dream symbols and came across the sun. After reading the definition, I was amazed by how much I felt it defined me and my outlook on life. Right there I adopted it as my official icon. I now wear it on charm bracelets and around my neck. It adorns my stationery and my office walls.

It never fails that someone notices and comments on my signature symbol, and it really does make me feel distinctive and warm. It is a constant reminder of the kind of woman I want to be: A woman who takes responsibility for making her own sunshine, and who is open and generous enough to allow others to bask in it as well. This knowledge of myself informs what I do and how I do it.

So think about the shape or symbol you've always been fascinated by. You don't have to worry about what someone else tells you it means; just recognize the positive emotions it brings out in you and let those feelings influence the way you see yourself and behave. Define yourself for the rest of the world, and then let the world get to know and love the sensual woman within.

SHOEBOX WISDOM
*Style is a simple way of saying
complicated things.*

—JEAN COCTEAU

Your wardrobe is definitely image defining. So every sensual woman should have her own *signature style*. Are you a fashionista or into the classics? Are you a girly girl or an earthy diva? Know your style preference and dress and accessorize to express it. Your clothes, shoes, and accessories should all work together to tell the world that you are a woman to be noticed and admired. This includes everything from a signature piece of jewelry to your signature lipstick color, fragrance, and cocktail.

The 19th-century fashion designer Lady Duff Gordon (queen of the slit skirt) once said, "Put even the plainest woman into a beautiful dress and she will try to live up to it." I don't disagree, but I feel the need to edit. Here's my spin on her comment: "Put any woman in a look that makes her feel good about who she is, and she will not only change, but flourish, and that's when her true beauty shines."

But your signature style doesn't begin with the visual image you present to the world. It starts with the very first pieces of clothing you pull on each morning—your *signature sexies*.

You should have your own signature look when it comes to your wardrobe down under, and even more than your outer clothing, your lingerie should make you feel lovely about being you. So often our outer wardrobe is dictated by the rules of our professional environment, but what you wear *under* your clothes speak volumes about how *you* see yourself as a woman. The conversation going on between your feminine psyche and your drawers can go two ways: 1) You identify and care about yourself as a woman, and sexy is who you are 24/7, not just when you're putting it into action; and 2) Well, let's just say it's the opposite of number one.

What is your underwear saying about you?

Lingerie has unfortunately become an iconic part of the *costume* we don when we are trying to *act* hot and sexy. And it is a strict SU policy that one never wears anything, undies included, for anyone other than oneself. Wearing your signature sexies has nothing to do with seducing a lover (the ogles and happy smiles are just a fabulous side perk) and everything to do with seducing you into believing, accepting, and behaving like the sensuous creature you are. Your sexies become a gentle daily reminder of who you are at your feminine core.

I've always loved pretty underwear because of the way it makes me feel about myself. It doesn't matter if I'm wearing a business suit, a cocktail dress, or sweats and a baggy old T-shirt, I've got on my signature sexies. They are my sexy secret and I wear them just for me. Anyone else I choose to share them with is simply a lucky beneficiary.

Now, before some of you get your knickers in a twist, understand that your signature sexies are no different from the other four sensual signatures you're identifying to define yourself as a confident, sensual woman. Just like your heel height, your sexies should be comfortable and should speak to your personal style sensibilities. So maybe you're a LaPerla girl, or Hanes for Her are more for you. Perhaps you connect to the look and feel of cotton, or maybe satin and lace are what get your eyes twinkling. Boy shorts or thongs, bikini or briefs, demi cup or sports bra—whatever your preference, just make sure your signature sexies are your brand of hot. Oh, and one very important point: don't ever leave your pretty things languishing in the bureau drawer waiting for a special occasion. Every day you walk this earth is a special day! So dress accordingly!

Finally, when you step out dressed under and over in your signature style, have a song in your heart. The Marines have one. So do the Army, Navy, and Air Force. Sports teams, celebrities, and presidential candidates all have theirs. I'm talking about a *signature fight song or theme song*. What's yours? What's the song that picks you up, makes you stand taller and turns your walk into a golden gait? The song that the woman within relates to; the one that makes her feel invincible when she hears the first few notes. Not the mommy. Not the wife. Not the lover. But the woman. This is the song that gets your juices flowing, puts a twist to your lips, a swing in your hips, and dares the world to ignore you.

So there you have them, the five sensual signatures that every woman with her Master of the Sensual Arts degree should own. Let's be clear. These are not items you save and bring out for special occasions. These are things you build your sensual persona around, the signatures people come to know you by. These are your personal touches that make you stand out in the crowd and mark you as a woman who knows and likes herself. You're not trying to dress up and play at being a sensual woman—you are owning your matchless sensuality and therefore simply being irresistibly yourself. Each item on this list should remind you, first and foremost, that you are a confident, distinctive, sensual woman; and by default, the rest of the world will realize this too.

EMBRACE MS. CHANGE
AND INVITE HER INTO YOUR LIFE

So, we've discussed the perfection of imperfection and the importance of branding yourself with your sensual signatures. Now the question must be asked: When was the last time you updated your look?

It's always a great idea to embrace change and invite her into your life. It's so very easy to get in a rut and let the familiar rule your life. The familiar is a known entity. It's comfortable. Familiar is easy and safe. It's what we know, and what for the most part has worked for years.

SHOEBOX WISDOM
Look your best. Who said love is blind?

—MAE WEST

But the familiar can also be stale. And boring. And a great place to hide. Often, what has been working for years no longer does, but it's part of our comfort zone and we'd rather hang on to what we know than risk something we don't. Keeping things the same holds us back from taking chances and venturing forth and finding out just how amazing the world is and what incredible women we have the potential to become.

I am a true believer in periodic makeovers. Just as there

is a necessity for the occasional attitude readjustment, every woman needs to undergo a style makeover now and again.

Your outer appearance is your calling card to the world and should reflect your most current inner self. If it doesn't, ask yourself why not. Do the two not match because you're hiding what's inside for fear of rejection, or do you not know the femme within? Are you allowing someone else in your life to dictate your first impression?

Our faces and figures change as time tiptoes on. What flattered the former you years ago probably doesn't do justice to the present you. If you haven't changed your look in years, it's time for an update. Here are a three makeover tips to get you going.

1. **Work on your five sensual signatures.** This will help ensure that your finished makeover is authentically you and not based on some celebrity ideal or fashion trend.

2. **Decide what you want.** Just wanting to "look better" is too general and can easily become an exercise in frustration. Divide your makeover goals into doable steps so you can prioritize your transformation and make it a happier, more manageable task.

3. **Start with the fast four: hair, makeup, teeth whitening, and posture.** These are generally budget-friendly items and the results are quick and encouraging. Start with these so you already feel fresh and fantastic as you work on other more time-consuming or costly things like diet and wardrobe.

▶ **HAIR:** Before you hit the salon, have an idea of what you hope to achieve. Look at photos of celebrities with similarly shaped faces, or go to a wig shop or websites like *InStyle* magazine's virtual makeover (www.instyle.com/instyle/makeover), where you can upload your photo and try on several hairstyles.

▶ **MAKEUP:** Sephora, MAC stores, and other cosmetic companies do in-store makeovers (some are complimentary). Let them show you a new, contemporary color palette to flatter your skin tone and bring out your most amazing facial feature.

▶ **TEETH:** Crest Whitestrips are a cost-effective way to get your smile bright and ready to showcase with a new lip color (certain lip colors can also make your teeth appear whiter). Of course, a bleached smile does not replace healthy gums and teeth. See your dentist regularly and brush and floss between appointments.

▶ **POSTURE:** Want to look like you've lost weight? Stand up straight. Practice standing tall with your shoulders back and your stomach pulled in. You'll be amazed at the instant lift to both your body and your self-esteem. It takes a while to train your core muscles, so when you feel yourself slouching, remind yourself to stand up straight and smile!

Change begets growth, and isn't that our ultimate job
in life—to grow? So invite Ms. Change into your life—and
grow into a stunning new version of you.

> ### I REALIZED THAT...
> "When you care about
> yourself it changes everything."
> Cathy '09

SOCIAL
WOW

CHAPTER FIVE

CF 105-INTRODUCTION TO CHARM AND FLIRTING

Whether in the bar, the boardroom, or the bedroom, every woman with her WOW should know how to charm and to "sell" herself—in a room full of strangers or alone with her beloved. Flirting is one of the great joys of being a woman. It puts the fizz in our social encounters and opens the door to countless opportunities to learn about our world and fall in love with the people who inhabit it. Sincere charm can change people's attitudes, turn a crisis into a comedy, and lighten the hearts that touch ours. And with practice, we can all be good at flirting. Yes, even you! I promise you, it's not as frightening as your imagination or past experiences have left you believing. Okay, I'm sure you noticed by now that I use the words

SHOEBOX WISDOM
Truth is a great flirt.

—FRANZ LISZT

charm and *flirting* interchangeably. I do this for two reasons:
First, because many women, particularly married women, get
caught deep in the lexis trap when it comes to the word *flirt*
or *flirting*, and "to charm" or "to be a charmer" has less of a
negative feel to them. Secondly, I interchange the words freely
because, in all the right ways, to flirt is to charm. So before
we go on, let's look at some of your feelings on the matter.

Questions 10 through 13 on your entrance exam were all
about judging yourself as a charmer. Question 10 asked you
to list three words to describe a woman who flirts. What
were yours? Were they negative or positive?

Which side of the trap you fall on tells you a lot about why
you are successful or unsuccessful at flirting. It's been my
experience that descriptive words for a woman who flirts fall
into two camps: 1) whore, loose, user, devious, gold digger,
bimbo, etc. 2) friendly, outgoing, confident, fun, popular. I
know, quite a disparity.

Question 11 asked what you personally thought about
flirting. Well? Is it a good thing? Do you find it easy to flirt with
strangers? What rating did you give yourself as a charmer?

The reason why women don't like to flirt or feel they aren't
good at it is usually the same. Their excuses may be different,

but it all boils down to the same thing: fear of rejection. And how in the world can anyone disagree? You are putting yourself out there to be judged, using covert and overt tactics to attract attention and make someone interested in you, to get them to see value in getting to know you better—how can you not be scared out of your newly acquired signature sexies?! So yes, with that mind-set, you have every right to be too scared to enjoy the idea of getting your flirt on.

SHOEBOX WISDOM
The basic thing which contributes to charm is the ability to forget oneself and be engrossed in other people.

—ELEANOR ROOSEVELT

Women who do like to charm and are good at it aren't necessarily any better looking than you, and they don't have better wardrobes or more to offer than you do. They just know the secret behind successful flirting: Flirting is a benevolent act. It is a gift of your time, appreciation, and interest that you give to others with no need, agenda, or desire to impress or win them over. And when you aren't looking to get anything, there is no reason to fear being rejected!

I love flirting. Flirting to me is as natural as breathing. I love to flirt because it makes me feel good. And powerful. And positive. Sometimes flirting makes me feel sexy, beautiful, and still relevant despite the fact that I am no longer in my physical prime. I flirt with people from all walks of life. I flirt with men, women, children, and animals. I flirt with strangers and friends alike, because the best part about flirting is knowing that I am making another person feel good about being who *they* are. In return, they make me feel good about being me. It's win–win for everybody!

And single ladies, what a man remembers is that he left feeling good about himself and you were the one who made him feel that way. All you wives out there who forgot, lost, or turned in your flirt card after you said, "I do": You need to pull that card out and dust it off.

SHOEBOX WISDOM
No matter how happily a woman may be married, it always pleases her to discover that there is a nice man who wishes that she were not.

—HENRY LOUIS MENCKEN

Many married women feel that innocent flirting with other men is a taboo activity left to single women. But what's really sad is that they even stop flirting with their mister. So let's flip the script and replace the word *flirting*, with all its hussy baggage, with the word *charm*, as in charming your mister.

It's not unusual for a woman to flirt in order to attract her man and then gradually dismiss her charming side as time, kids, and familiarity take over. But every woman should keep her sensual, charming self active and alive, both with her husband and others. Why? Here are three great reasons:

1. To maintain your sexual relevance as time goes by. Age is no longer a threat to your sexual confidence.
2. Because sexual confidence gives you a sense of control over your own destiny. No more thinking, *No other man will ever want me.*
3. To avoid the "intimacy" leak that siphons off marital passions.

Flirting with your husband is a crucial part of a married woman's arsenal. Flirting helps keep romance and playfulness alive in your marriage. It should not stop at the altar, nor should it stop at your 25th wedding anniversary.

Oh, and the best part, aside from making other people feel good about themselves? The happy fallout from being friendly and positive is that good things do come your way. I've gotten out of traffic tickets, been upgraded from an inside cabin to a suite on a cruise ship, and to first class on an airplane. I've drunk my fair share of complimentary beverages and meals, and I've come out on top at job interviews. But by being charming I've also met people who helped me professionally, who introduced me to others with skills and services I was in need of. I've met people who have become lifelong friends and others who were meant to be in my life for just a short time. And many times, flirting brought me in touch with people who needed me and my skills.

So, back to my original statement. With practice, we can all be good at flirting. Lead with your natural charisma, and unleash your own charm offensive.

EXAM

Just what kind of charmer are you? Here's a quick test to help you determine your natural flirting style.

1) What's your most important flirting tool?
a) Your body.
b) Your personality.
c) Your smile.
d) Not sure if you have one.

2. The last touch you add before leaving for a party is:
a) Glossy lipstick that draws attention to your mouth.
b) A funky, quirky handbag.
c) A charm bracelet that sparkles and jingles when you gesture.
d) A breath mint.

3. You see a man you'd like to meet. You:
a) Sit where he can see and enjoy your come-hither eye contact.
b) Pass him a joke sans punch line, with the suggestion that he come over to hear the rest.
c) Have a friend go tell him you'd like to meet him.
d) Wait until he leaves and ask a friend later who the person was.

4. **You and your lover are sitting across from each other at dinner. He is seductively maintaining eye contact. What do you do?**
a) Immediately ask for the check and get to a private place ASAP.
b) Hold his gaze and seduce him right back before playfully sticking out your tongue.
c) Stare back for a while, smile seductively to let him know you're feeling him, and then look away.
d) Start talking so he'll stop staring. All that gawking is uncomfortable.

5. **A man offers to buy you a drink. You ask for:**
a) A Sex on the Beach.
b) The same beer he's having.
c) Wine—it's flirty and sophisticated, but not too showy.
d) Tell him no thanks, and buy your own. You don't want to owe anyone anything.

Add it up. How many:
A's_____ B's_____ C's _____ D's_____

THE FLIRT FACTOR: YOUR FLIRTING STYLE

SEXY FLIRT (Mostly A's): You're a woman who sees what she wants and takes it. You've got all the right tools in your bag of tricks, and you know the signs and signals to attract what you want when you want it. In the right dose, you are pure power. Be careful about taking your sexy flirtation too far. Being too sexually overt can cause a multitude of things to occur; you can embarrass yourself, make other women dislike you, and make promises you don't intend to keep.

AMUSING FLIRT (Mostly B's): Your allure is your quick wit and wicked sense of humor. You can feel at home in a sports bar or at a poker game. You entice a man by making him feel comfortable around you. And though your "buddy" approach is less direct than those of other women, it can be just as disarming. By not playing the games other girls play, you lower his guard, and before he knows it, he's hooked. But watch that you don't become one of the boys. Find ways to let him know there is a lusty woman behind the ponytail.

CUTE FLIRT (Mostly C's): You've got a sparkle about you that attracts attention as soon as you enter a room, but you prefer not to be too aggressive when you meet a man who interests you. Instead, you tend to take the subtler approach to your seduction, letting him know you're interested, but letting him initiate the pursuit. With this light approach, know exactly what you want so your feelings are clear to him, or some other devastating diva might walk off with your man.

FLIRTING FLOP (Mostly D's): You're flirtability quotient is dangerously low. Lack of confidence may be the enemy lurking within. Remember: Flirting is a benevolent act. Concentrate on making people in your presence feel special, and it's goodbye rejection, hello charming you! Feel your confidence soar as your charm begins to disarm those around you. Now get out there and practice. You'll be successfully flirting in no time.

CHAPTER SIX

TW 106-TURN ON THE WOW
Lesson 1

For the past few weeks you've worked on uncovering your individual sensuality. Today we take the next step in bringing out the sensual you in a social setting: learning how to interact on a joyfully flirtatious level. This week, as you continue to build your WOW factor, you will also begin to dust off those atrophied womanly wiles. You start by learning to first charm and seduce yourself!

LECTURE: *Turn on the charm.* We were all born to charm. If you've ever watched a baby work the room with sparkling eyes, an irresistible smile, and sweet coos, you already know that charm is an inherent part of our DNA. So why is it so difficult to continue in adulthood what came so naturally during childhood? Why is it so hard to let the world see you in all your enchanting glory?

SHOEBOX WISDOM
Charm is a glow within a woman that casts a most becoming light on others.

—JOHN MASON BROWN

It's hard because you don't own *it*, it being the true essence of who you are. And if it isn't truly yours, how can you work it with any pride of ownership?

Oscar Wilde once wrote, "She behaves as if she was beautiful. Most American women do. It is the secret of their charm." This man was a genius of observation. Back in the 19th century, Oscar knew a basic truth that most of us have managed to forget: truly beautiful women make the most of their appearance, but also their personalities. Today, we live in a society where most women are too busy obsessing over their lack of celebrity smoke-and-mirrors perfection to fully recognize, and claim, what they already have in their possession.

So, how do you begin to own and operate your killer charm? Begin by believing in the power of being uniquely you.

PROFESSOR'S NOTES

Good posture does more than just signal that a confident, balanced woman has entered the room. It keeps your body functioning properly and gives you a feeling of pride and confidence. Plus, as a true gift from God, it makes you look taller and thinner!

Your posture influences many other body parts, and even a small imbalance in your posture can cause strain on your muscles. (This I know from experience!)

So stand tall and glide on!

DAILY FIELD TRIP: Continue your daily 20- to 60-minute walks with thoughtful emphasis on your posture. Confident women stand tall and walk with joyful knowledge that they own *it*, and that life is theirs for the taking.

TODAY'S WALKING THOUGHT: Listen to your signature song while you walk and let the message soak into your psyche.

CLASS ASSIGNMENT: Think about this question as you go about your day today. What would you do differently in your pursuit of a fulfilled love life if you accepted that you are just fine as you are? If you woke up to find that you looked and felt about yourself the way you always wanted to, how would your life change? In your journal, make a list of all the things you'd do differently and ways you'd behave differently than you do at this moment.

For this entire week, I want you to challenge yourself to accept the fact that you are perfectly amazing as is. Each time you find fault with your appearance or personality, you'll stop and remind yourself that you are fabulous and desirable right now. Then go out and behave as if you are beautiful, and see what happens.

NOTE-TAKING: Each day, record how you do with this challenge. Remember, there are moments in life when it's necessary to pretend till you win. Trust me, before you know it, pretending becomes believing, which begets the emergence of your true essence. Write about how far away you are from reaching this goal at this point, and what challenges are keeping you from being the charmer you are meant to be.

EXERCISE: Continue with three sets of 10 kegels, three times a day. Hum a stanza from your signature song while you kegel. If you have trouble with your kegels, strengthen those muscles by pressing a large rubber ball between your knees for the count of five. Repeat 10 times.

Lesson 2

LECTURE: *EBS (Evil Bitch Syndrome).* How often do you display EBS without even meaning to? How many times has some man (even yours) said hello or called out a compliment (not in a rude or obnoxious way but sincerely and appreciatively) or asked you to dance at a club—and you've rolled your eyes, sucked your teeth, given him your "No, you didn't" look, and kept on walking as if he'd just said you had a unibrow?

PROFESSOR'S NOTES

If you only knew how few people really are looking to judge you and pounce on your weaknesses, you'd probably spend a lot more time feeling cheerful and positive about yourself and your life and less time judging others.

The only person who is in constant judgment of you is *you.*

Women treat well-meaning strangers this way time after time and then wonder why a good and attentive man is so hard to find. And they can't understand why men think women are so full of 'tude.

Why do we fall into this behavior? Because many times we are so busy judging the person giving us the compliment as unworthy or undesirable, or questioning his motives, that we *can't hear the validation of our worthiness.*

True, you won't be attracted to every man who approaches you. But learn to accept flattering comments from a man who just wants to let you know he recognizes quality when he sees it; it is just another opportunity for you to practice letting loose your genuine power smile and basking in some unexpected admiration.

And remember the oh-so-important law of attraction: energy attracts like energy. So if you insist on walking around spreading EBS just because you can, expect to attract men with NAC (Nasty Attitude Complex) growling right back at you!

DAILY FIELD TRIP: On your 20- to 60-minute walk today, concentrate on projecting a friendly and approachable demeanor.

TODAY'S WALKING THOUGHT: Listen to your signature song and be inspired. Continue walking tall, and feel beautiful!

CLASS ASSIGNMENT: This week, pay constant attention to your attitude and facial expressions. Do they match? If you are in a good mood, does your face and body language transmit it, or do you find that you are suffering from chronic EBS even when your mood dictates the opposite? Cure yourself of EBS by staying in touch with your Fan Five as you go about your day. Your face will translate the intake of delight around you.

I REALIZED THAT...
"I had a bad case of EBS when I was out with some of my friends and a guy told me that it was such a shame that a face so pretty should look so mean. And I wasn't even in a bad mood!"
Talia '07

In addition to paying attention to your body and facial language, let's add this to your challenge: Today, instead of constantly evaluating, labeling and analyzing everything and everybody, you will practice being nonjudgmental. By constantly passing judgment, you are creating a lot of internal turbulence and giving credence to your negative thoughts about yourself and others (and increasing your EBS). So try to observe and experience the people you meet today but keep yourself from judging them in any way and feeling that they are judging you. Continue to extend this judgment-free zone to yourself as well. Truly sexy women, while they make judgments about people, are never *judgmental*.

Try adopting this as your mantra today: "It is what it is. And it's all good."

NOTE-TAKING: At the end of the day, spend some time journaling about how it felt not to judge or allow yourself to be judged. Did you find the experience difficult, or empowering? Limiting, or liberating? What are your feelings about this experiment? Also, explore your EBS. How badly do you suffer from it?

EXERCISE: Continue with three sets of 10 kegels, three times a day. Hum a stanza from your signature song while you kegel.

Lesson 3

LECTURE: *Your inner diva.* We all have one. She's the niggling voice you hear telling you to let loose and go for it. She's the one encouraging you to step out of your boring comfort zone and into the spotlight. She's the hottie who shares all your moral integrity and values, but also gives voice to your own truth. She's your inner diva. Let the bold, confident girl breathe. She has an important role to play in your sensual life.

PROFESSOR'S NOTES

Continue to apply last week's attitude of gratitude to all your assignments this week.

Don't forget your challenge from the past two lessons! Remember, it doesn't work if you accept yourself and others once and then go back to your old ways. You've got to tend and maintain your charming self just the way you would a great new haircut.

Feeling a little unsure about this whole idea of bringing to life your alter ego? Well, even one of the sexiest women in the world fell back on her inner diva to give her some self-assurance when she needed it. Yes, Beyoncé Knowles, aka Sasha Fierce. Years ago, while in her early twenties, Beyoncé created Sasha in an effort to separate her own shy personality from her stage persona and give her the courage to be free and sexy while performing. Yep, even international superstars are pretending till they win! In 2010, Beyoncé announced that she was now comfortable enough with herself to be sexy and daring all on her own. "I don't need Sasha Fierce anymore, because I've grown and now I am able to merge the two."

And just like Beyoncé, there will come a time when you no longer need to fall back on your alter ego. But until then, unearth your inner diva and let her help unleash the WOW in you.

DAILY FIELD TRIP: On your 20- to 60-minute walk today, take your inner diva out for a stroll.

TODAY'S WALKING THOUGHT: Continue to listen to your song. Walk tall, as if you believe you are beautiful.

CLASS ASSIGNMENT: Sit in your sanctuary with your journal and think about your inner diva. Bring her to life. Write about her and get to know her. Give her a name. What does she like to eat and drink? What is her philosophy about life and love? What are her sexual likes and dislikes? What is her personal motto? Describe her attitude and demeanor. Think about attention that makes you feel vulnerable and uncomfortable—how does it make her feel? How does she handle it?

It is important to understand that you are not creating a fictional character. You are acknowledging a part of yourself that you have kept hidden and under wraps for any number of reasons. You are bringing into balance the inner diva you left behind as you nurtured the more comfortable and confident sides of yourself—the professional, the friend, the daughter, the mother, and so on.

For the rest of the semester (and beyond), every time you

find yourself in a social/sexual situation where you feel willing but still shy and uncomfortable, smile and think to yourself: What would [insert diva name here] do? And act accordingly. Access her when needed and bless her for helping you become the wholly fantastic woman you are meant to be.

NOTE-TAKING: In your journal, record your thoughts about the idea of acknowledging and releasing your inner diva. How does the suggestion make you feel? Silly? Excited? Fraudulent? Supported? Really investigate your thoughts so you are able to follow through with maximum success. Think about this hidden side of yourself. Who banished her from your everyday life? Your parents? Lovers? Religious beliefs? How does it feel to set her free? Liberating, or frightening? Why?

EXERCISE: Continue with three sets of 10 kegels, three times a day. Let your inner diva control your thoughts while you kegel.

Lesson 4

LECTURE: *What do you want?* Finding and being your charming self with everyone you meet is essential to living happily on your own terms. But as you begin to amp up your vamp, particularly if you are in the market to add a partner to your life, it's also important to be concerned first and foremost with what *you* want in a man. We spend so much of our time worrying about being worthy and wondering why nobody seems to want us, we have no idea what is really important to us when it comes down to the nitty-gritty of love. We scour magazines and the Internet looking for clues to what men want and how we can become that girl so they will pick us. In our desire to "be what he wants," most of us are willing to change ourselves and deny our own needs for the sake of having someone in our lives. When we do this, we forget two important facts: 1) You *are* something special, damn it! and 2) Happiness is truly fleeting if you deny yourself and your truth. Because really, no man—no matter his looks, personality, or wealth—will make you happy if he is ultimately not what *you* want.

PROFESSOR'S NOTES

It's time to lose the mentality that the quality of your life and love is based on his choices. Take your power back! Don't wait for him to pick you! When it comes to finding the energy you want to drive your life, be the decider. You do that by improving yourself and the quality of love you have to offer, being open to choices that appear, and allowing your positive energy to flow.

DAILY FIELD TRIP: Today, walk with the intention of worthiness.

TODAY'S WALKING THOUGHT: *I am who I think I am, and I think I'm* _____ .

CLASS ASSIGNMENT: Make your list. When you have the time, sit in your sanctuary and think about what you want in your mate. Don't get caught up in the superficial—what he looks like, how much money he makes, how he dresses, where he was educated, what part of town he lives in, what kind of car he drives, etc. None of those things count in the long run. Concentrate on the personality qualities, morals, and values that are deal breakers for you. For example, if I were back in the market, my list would look like this:

> Must be: educated, responsible, and well employed. Funny, flexible, independent, passionate, kind, and confident. Deal breakers: addictions, jealousy, negative energy, inability to get along with my children.

Everything on my list is based on my knowledge of myself. Anything else positive he brings to the party is gravy. Anything else negative will be reviewed and sorted and his future in my life to be determined.

> **I REALIZED THAT...**
> "The reason I didn't want the men I was getting was because all the things I said I wanted weren't important. Finally, I have my priorities straight!"
> Virginia '07

Take a look at your list of gentle demands. Is it reasonable? Would you be capable of meeting your own needs? Does it demand more of a mate than it does of yourself? Take a moment to focus on what you want. Once you've done that, you've taken the first step in creating it.

ASSIGNMENT #2: *Creative visualization.* Escape to your sanctuary for at least 10 minutes, where you won't be disturbed. Get in a comfortable position, whether sitting or lying down. Relax your body completely. Breathe deeply and slowly and release all tension in your body.

When you feel deeply relaxed, start to imagine the woman you want to be in a social situation. Locate your fantasy man (whether he's your real man or one you've got on order) and go meet him. Imagine yourself being the charming, flirtatious, interesting woman you are.

Now, keeping this image still in your mind, say positively and affirmatively to yourself (aloud or silently, whatever you prefer): "I am a confident, charming woman who knows what she wants and knows how to get it." Always end your visualization with the following: "This, or something better, now manifests for me in totally harmonious ways, for the good of all concerned."

NOTE-TAKING: Jot down in your journal what you would be like without the fear of rejection dictating your every mood. Next, make a list of the men you have experienced in your life. What do they have in common? Put a circle around the great ones. What qualities did you love about each of them? Put an X next to the ones whose negative qualities dominate your memories. Jot them down. Use this information as insight to the kind of man you're attracted to and his pleasing qualities. If your negative list outweighs the positive, think about what this says about the energy you are putting out into the world.

EXERCISE: Continue with three sets of 10 kegels, three times a day.

Lesson 5

LECTURE: *Body language.* Just as EBS and facial expressions can be an intimidating turn-off, and a charming *don't,* so can your body language. Last week we worked on conveying confidence by walking with better posture. But what message is the rest of your body sending without your knowledge or consent? What are you conveying to the world about your availability, approachability, and feminine confidence through the way you stand, walk, and sit? Your body language reveals a lot about you. Your facial expressions and body gestures are the first things people notice—even if they don't consciously realize it. Before you utter a single word, your mannerisms, no matter how subtle, send a message that's loud and clear. Your posture, how you hold your arms, what your eyes focus on—these all speak volumes.

For example: Crossing your arms in front of your chest gives off a "Stay away from me/I'm not worthy of your attention" vibe. Certain movements don't belong on your social face. These include licking your lips, tightening your jaw, frowning, and twitching.

HERE ARE SOME TIPS TO REMEMBER:

▸ When you shake hands, be firm, not wimpy or overly enthusiastic.

▸ When you sit, stay tall and find a comfortable legs-crossed position. Check out the talk show hosts. That's how you want to look when you sit.

▸ Want to seem friendly? Turn fully toward the other person.

▸ Always stand with your shoulders back, and head up. (Don't slouch!)

DAILY FIELD TRIP: Continue your daily 20- to 60-minute walks with thoughtful emphasis on your body language today. This week, add an additional five minutes to your walking—indoors, in the highest heels you find comfortable. Practice a graceful, seductive glide that ends with you seated in a chair in a posture-perfect, leg-flattering position. Tip: Throw on your heels (and your inner diva) while you're getting ready in the morning.

TODAY'S WALKING THOUGHT: Today, as you walk, think of one endearing quality about your mate or the man you want from your list that you want to bring into your life.

CLASS ASSIGNMENT: Spend time in your closet this week putting together your WOW wear—the outfit that flatters your body type, enhances your best features, and makes you feel fabulous. Build this outfit around your sexiest pair of shoes.

NOTE-TAKING: What did you learn about your body language and the way you approach the world? Has being mindful of your body language had any impact on the way others view and respond to you?

Record your thoughts about the endearing quality of the man you love or the one you want. Why is this quality important to you and how does it make you feel about yourself and him?

EXERCISE: Continue with three sets of 10 kegels, three times a day.

Extra Credit

If you can get by a shoe store any day this week, spend some time trying on sexy shoes. Find the style that looks most flattering on your feet and legs. Experiment with different vamps, heel lengths, and strap variations. And, yes, while comfort is very important, remember that these aren't the shoes you'll be wearing to grocery-shop or work in all day. These are part of your "grown and sexy" shoe collection—shoes designed to literally lift you up and turn you on. It doesn't matter whether you buy a pair today or not. Your goal here is to find the right shoe for your Cinderella nights.

Week six is coming to an end. Hopefully you're feeling more sensual and confident about the woman you are ultimately becoming. Give yourself a grade based on the amount of work you did this week and how well you applied the lessons learned.

TW 106 CLASS GRADE:

_____

CHAPTER SEVEN

SELL 107-S.E.L.L. YOURSELF
Lesson 1

It's flirt week at Stiletto University! You're now nearly halfway through your Stiletto U semester. During these past few weeks, I hope you have become acquainted and besotted with your newly emerging sensual self. Today we begin to take the next steps toward unleashing this more confident, vibrant, charming you, not only onto the world but onto the men in your life who matter most. This week, as you continue to explore your God-given girl skills, you will also begin to practice S.E.L.L.ing yourself.

LECTURE: *Social sensuality.* With practice, we can all be good at flirting. Flirting takes no special equipment and costs nothing. Your God-given attributes will do you just fine. A good flirt is merely a woman who has learned to revel in the power of being a woman, is determined to enjoy herself in the moment, and has a benevolent streak. Yes, a benevolent streak, because successful flirting is all about transferring your good feelings onto others, making them feel good about being themselves around *you*. Flirting begins and ends with feminine confidence. So if you stop looking at being charming and flirtatious as a method of *getting* something or impressing someone, and instead look at it as a way of *giving* something and complimenting someone, you will lose your fear of rejection and gain a friendly sense of approachability. You will be surprised how people respond to you in all situations—and how often you will get your way.

PROFESSOR'S NOTES
The key to being successfully charming is to stop worrying about yourself and start being curious about the other folks in the room.

DAILY FIELD TRIP: Today, on your daily 20- to 60-minute walk, practice being friendly, open, and curious with the humans, animals, and plants you come across.

TODAY'S WALKING THOUGHT: Walk as if you are the subject being sung about in your signature song.

CLASS ASSIGNMENT: Give and you shall receive. Reap what you sow. Common proverbs and all around good advice. Kindness begets kindness. Interest begets interest. Love begets love. Another way to say it: What goes out must come back. So what are you putting out in the social circles of your life and receiving in return?

This week, wherever you go and whomever you encounter, give them a gift. It can be a compliment, a genuine smile, money in their parking meter, a silent prayer. Silently wish them joy, happiness, and laughter. Make an effort to accept with gratitude all the gifts you receive in return.

This is the true power of WOW—bestowing your positive energy, concern, and interest on someone else and accepting theirs in return.

ASSIGNMENT #2: Take some quiet time to reexamine the results of your flirt test. Are you surprised by the outcome? Are you comfortable with the suggested analysis of your flirt style? If not, list various ways that you put into action your flirtatious behavior. If you are surprised, try to figure out the source of the disconnect between how you feel and how you act.

NOTE-TAKING: Think back to one of your *least* successful attempts to be charming and flirtatious. Write down all you can remember about how the event transpired. Try to recapture your emotions about the situation. Now consider your most successful flirting attempt to date. What happened? How did you feel about yourself? What was different about you, the man, and the situation? What do you think made the difference between failure and success?

EXERCISE: Continue with three sets of 10 kegels, three times a day. Think charming thoughts while you kegel.

Lesson 2

LECTURE: *S.E.L.L. yourself.* Now that you understand the core attitude to mounting a successful charm offensive, it's time to learn the basic, no-fail techniques.

Smile—often and naturally. It's amazing that we really don't pay much attention to how much we *don't* smile. Smiling is our most effective calling card, a free and easy spirit lifter, and a surefire antidote to negative energy. **A genuine smile is power.** With it you can change another person's entire mood and perspective, as well as your own. Smiling makes you look friendly, confident, and approachable, and puts the other person at ease. And if he's feeling at ease, he's bound to be more receptive and interested in you. Note: A genuine smile is one where eyes and mouth work together.

PROFESSOR'S NOTES
S.E.L.L. Yourself
Smile
Eyes
Listen
Laugh

This week, practice selling yourself to *everybody*, not just the objects of your desire.

DAILY FIELD TRIP: Today you will continue with your daily 20- to 60-minute walk and your 10-minute high-heel session. Smile!

TODAY'S WALKING THOUGHT: Focus on yet another personality quality that attracted you to your man or the man in your future.

CLASS ASSIGNMENT: Smiling is contagious. And in a flirting situation, we want to infect as many folks as possible. It's your job to infect as many people as you can today with your genuine smile. For the rest of the week, pay constant attention to your facial expression and practice smiling. If you're waiting in a cashier's line, smile. When you pass strangers on the street, smile. Smile when you notice a beautiful flower or the clear blue sky. Make it a habit, and soon you will find yourself not only happier and more persuasive but on the receiving end with greater frequency.

Begin smiling while you speak on the phone, particularly when talking with your mate or someone you're interested in or trying to do business with. Be particularly aware of how their tone of voice changes during your conversation. The other person can feel and hear the difference in your voice. There is a warmth and friendliness that comes across with a grin.

MIDTERM EXAM: Make plans for a date this weekend with your man or with a girlfriend to go somewhere where plenty of people are around. This date is less a romantic interlude and more a fun escapade to let you test your flirty charming skills. Do what you have to do—clear schedules, hire a babysitter—to make this happen.

NOTE-TAKING: How do you feel about your smile? What does it looks like? What shape is it in? When was the last time you saw your dentist? What can you do to enhance your smile both cosmetically and medically (a cleaning, perhaps)?

Jot down in your journal how your mood or your life was affected this week by the mere act of smiling. How did those around you react to your smiles?

EXERCISE: Continue with three sets of 10 kegels, three times a day. You guessed it! Smile while you kegel.

Lesson 3

LECTURE: *Eye contact/Talk.* Your eyes are your most important flirting tool. It's important to start cultivating your looks as part of your charming style because when trying to draw a man over to your side of the room or keep him at the table next to you, an interested set of eyes and a warm smile will rarely let you down. Note: If your smile doesn't reach your eyes, you'll appear bored and disingenuous.

I REALIZED THAT...
"I'd been walking around with dead eyes. It thrills me to enliven through my eyes. It makes such a difference in engaging and connecting with others."
Gigi '09

Once you've captured someone's attention with your smile and have him locked into your gaze, let your eyes communicate all the things you'd love to say but feel too silly or forward verbalizing. Drown him in unspoken compliments and he will start living to spend time in your gaze. Married ladies, this is a great game to play with your spouse. Tease his imagination with things left unsaid and he'll be putty in your hands trying to break the code.

DAILY FIELD TRIP: Today, on your 20- to 60-minute walk, see if you can catch someone's gaze and give him an eyeful!

TODAY'S WALKING THOUGHT: Focus today on the one attribute you find sexiest about your man or the man of your future.

CLASS ASSIGNMENT: Practice eye-talking with the people in your life (your man, kids, friends, co-workers). Using only your eyes, communicate the positive, loving things you usually say; other things you're too embarrassed to say; or things you've been dying to say.

EXERCISE: Make eye play part of your morning routine. As you're getting ready for your day, practice flirting with yourself. Look in the mirror and hold your own gaze. Practice complimenting yourself through eye talk. Smile and witness your mesmerizing effect. It may seem silly at first, but better now, alone with yourself, than out in public. Keep practicing until flirting and smiling with your eyes becomes second nature.

NOTE-TAKING: In your journal, make a list of people you notice who use their eyes as charm magnets. Here are a few to get you started: Elizabeth Taylor, Johnny Depp, Prince, Alicia Keys.

Write down your thoughts about how your ocular conversations went. What kind of reactions did you get? Do you think your facial expressions translated your thoughts accurately?

EXERCISE: Continue with three sets of 10 kegels, three times a day.

Lesson 4

LECTURE: *Listen.* Your ability to listen effectively is the secret to coming off completely fascinating to people. The more you listen and ask questions, the more attractive, mysterious, and intriguing you become. Asking for more details proves you have been paying attention, and sends the message that you find him interesting. Don't think too hard about what you're going to say—just really listen to what he is saying and respond naturally.

Listening also helps keep the power (KTP) in your hands because it gives you the opportunity to *learn*. People give many clues about themselves during a conversation. If you take the time, you'll find out things that help you decide if this conversation is "To be continued" or "Nice meeting you, have a great life." Either way, it's lady's choice.

When you've been listening to the same voice for years, your hearing can become conveniently selective. Tune back in to your mate and start listening again with your ears and heart. Consider a little appointment time on the couch with the TV off, or a weekly drink dedicated strictly to getting your ears on each other again. You'll be surprised what you learn and the positive impact it can have on your relationship.

DAILY FIELD TRIP: Enjoy your 20- to 60-minute walk. Walk proud, with the knowledge that you have made great strides these past weeks and you're only getting better!

TODAY'S WALKING THOUGHT: Listen to your heart about the ways your mate (or child, family member, or some other special person) adds joy to your life.

CLASS ASSIGNMENT: Be in the moment in every conversation you have today, particularly with those you love and live with. This includes co-workers, strangers, boyfriends, spouses, and children. Are you hearing or noticing anything about them that you hadn't before? What did you learn new about someone today?

MIDTERM EXAM: Finalize plans and wardrobe for your outing this weekend. Make sure it is flattering and above all that it is comfortable, both physically and emotionally. The last thing you want to be worrying about is your dress/spanks riding up or your pants being too tight. It's never a bad idea to have a go-to, never lets me down outfit that always makes you feel great about being you.

NOTE-TAKING: What did you learn this week about others and yourself through effective listening? What do you think is the difference between hearing and listening to someone?

Are you a good listener? Do you listen and really hear, or are you simply letting them have their say and waiting for them to finish so you can make your point? Have you ever experienced someone not listening to you? How did you feel?

EXERCISE: Continue with three sets of 10 kegels, three times a day.

Lesson 5

LECTURE: *Laugh.* When you're in charm mode, if you're not listening or talking, you should be laughing. Laughter and humor are also powerful armaments in your seductive artillery. It's almost impossible to flirt successfully and enjoyably without them. So don't be afraid of engaging in a little playful jousting , but remember that you walk a very fine line between wit and sarcasm.

Stay away from giggling. Giggling translates into anxiety, and you are a cool and confident woman, not a teenager on her first date.

PROFESSOR'S NOTES

As you concentrate on these individual S.E.L.L. techniques, don't forget to practice them together in order to reap their most powerful benefits.

DAILY FIELD TRIP: Today, on your 20- to 60-minute walk, stride with flirtatious intent. This really means nothing more than walking tall and confidently with an approachable, friendly aura about you. Tonight, take those heels on a stroll and really work it.

TODAY'S WALKING THOUGHT: *I am the new sexy.*

CLASS ASSIGNMENT: Combine your S.E.L.L. techniques and practice throughout the day on everyone in preparation for your date this weekend.

ASSIGNMENT #2: For your midterm excursion, here are a few DON'Ts to keep in mind.

▶ DON'T take it too seriously. The most successful flirts are those who enjoy it and can flirt without expecting anything to come of it. Leave the "must score" attitude at home or you risk looking desperate. Practice charming men whom you aren't interested in, and soon you'll be able to flirt with the one you adore and still appear casual.

▶ Flirt, DON'T tease. There is a difference between innocent flirting and a full-court come-on. Avoid overtly sexual talk or touching. Be mysterious—show your interest by being friendly, but don't offer more than you intend to give. Consider this when you are choosing your attire. Suggestive and revealing clothing says less about you being a powerful, sensual woman and more about you being sexually available.

▶ DON'T be unkind. If someone you are not interested in approaches you, act appreciative and polite. Remember, he is only gifting you with his admiration. Smile and be friendly before discouraging further contact. Let him leave with his pride intact. Other men are watching to see what you do. If you laugh after he leaves or show visual disapproval, you are lessening your chances of anyone else approaching you. And besides, it's just not nice.

NOTE-TAKING: Jot down in your journal how you feel about what you are manifesting in your life. How did things go this week? Did you find it easy to put your charm into action? How did your date/event go? Was it easy? Fun? Productive? Or difficult and painful?

EXERCISE: Continue with three sets of 10 kegels, three times a day.

Week seven is coming to an end. Hopefully you're feeling more sensual and confident about the woman you are ultimately becoming. Give yourself a grade based on the amount of work you did this week and how well you applied the lessons learned.

SELL 107 CLASS GRADE:

_____

CHAPTER EIGHT

CLL 108-CHARMED LIVING LABORATORY

This week you will put the lessons of the last two weeks into practice and solidify your newfound sense of social sensuality.

LECTURE: The ability to charm and disarm is a priceless skill, useful in myriad situations. The trick is to lose your fear of rejection and the worry that you are being judged. In this unit, we've worked on incorporating charm into your daily life, and incorporating everyone you encounter, not just those you are interested in.

PROFESSOR'S NOTES

Flirting is a benevolent act. This you now know. You also know that you won't be interested in every man who crosses your rose-petal path, and neither will every man be interested in you. With this in mind, it's important for you to have a gentle, friendly exit line for those who don't spark your interest, but who gift you with their attention.

Mine?

"My husband *really* hates when I date, but thanks so much. You've made an old married lady very happy tonight."

Delivered, of course, with a killer smile!

EVIL BITCH SYNDROME: There is a saying I remember from my youth, "Check yourself before you wreck yourself." Sage advice. Look at some of your important relationships and see how bad you're suffering from EBS. The cure: Smile, be in touch with your Fan Five, and let positivity reign.

S.E.L.L. YOURSELF: Make a real effort to incorporate your S.E.L.L. techniques in all your daily interactions. Practice on the guy at the gas station, your child's teacher, a co-worker, a stranger on the street, or your spouse and family.

CLASS ASSIGNMENT: Discover and revel in your ability to touch and brighten someone else's life just by sharing your charming self with them. Gift the people you encounter with a smile, a compliment, or a silent wish for love and light. When you are in giving mode, it is impossible to look, feel, or act evil.

Catch up on any assignments you didn't get to or would

like to repeat from the last two weeks. Continue to revel in your sensual world through your Fantabulous Five, and work on putting your Sensual Signatures in place.

I REALIZED THAT...
"Just making small changes like taking better care of myself, dressing for my body, and wearing matching undies has made a huge difference. I have more good days now than bad days. My husband is now happy that I'm happy."
Lauren '08

NOTE-TAKING: Take time to record your thoughts and feelings about what you learned this week about yourself through your social world and living sensuously.

EXERCISE: Bump up your kegels to three sets of 15 kegels, three times a day.

MIDTERM EXAM: This weekend's date/event is your practical midterm exam. It's time to mark your progress. Journal your thoughts, delights, and doubts about how things went.

Extra Credit:

TURN ON THE WOW MOVIE SUGGESTIONS

Here are two more favorite selections from the Stiletto University movie vault. These two present the social sensuality concepts you've been working on in this unit in an East-meets-West show of feminine confidence. Pass the popcorn!

THE THOMAS CROWN AFFAIR. I like both versions, the classic and the remake, but I am particularly drawn to the Pierce Brosnan and Renee Russo version (the remake). This is a sexy cat-and-mouse game that showcases a strong, confident, sexy woman of a certain age who still remains vulnerable and feminine. The soundtrack is awesome and the love scene in the entry and study is truly inspirational!

MEMOIRS OF A GEISHA. This film is a visually stunning adaptation of the best-selling book and is luxurious, ethereal and intoxicating. And to top it off, it has many lessons to teach about enticement and the power of seduction. The scene where Sayuri is taught how to stop a man in his tracks with one look is priceless and proves that true charm is indeed an international affair.

The Philosophy of WOW

LOSE THE MOTH MENTALITY, LIGHT YOUR FLAME

I've always had a motto about men. Simply put, "Let them be the moths; I am the flame." As I look back and try to figure out when and where this notion got planted in my head, I can only come up with my parents. I mean, they never said such a thing, but their rules ultimately shaped my thoughts and actions.

I wasn't allowed to date until I was 16 (couldn't even have phone calls from boys until I was 15), so aggressively pursuing a boy or even looking for a boyfriend was a moot point. Of course, I was too mortified to tell boys that my house rules were so strict, so I developed a knack for turning them down nicely and went about the business of developing my own interests. In the process, I also developed an air of friendly nonchalance that apparently proved to be intriguing.

Despite the fact that I thought my parents were brutally unkind, now I see that I actually learned three valuable lessons in those early years: 1) boys like a bit of a chase; 2) staying busy doing my own thing—whether work or play— was a good thing because having my own life and interests is an important part of any relationship; and 3) boys will always find you, especially when you're not looking.

So be the flame.

Being the flame gives you a very positive attitude to wrap your mind around. (And we all know, where your mind goes, your butt follows.) Flame glows. Flame attracts. Flame lights the way and warms the path. Flame welcomes and mesmerizes. Flame is white hot!

Be the flame, because when you're the moth, you simply become one of several flitting around someone else's light, waiting and hoping that you'll get noticed (and increasing your chances of getting burned). When you're the moth, you give the flame the power to pick and choose; to validate and make you feel attractive and wanted. Bump that—*Be the flame!*

I know, easier said than done. Well, let's talk about a few ways to make sure your flame burns big and bright enough to attract the moths with the right stuff.

1. **Change your attitude, change your life.** Stop living with the moth mentality and let your light shine. Stop believing that basking in the light of some man's flame will make you happy, and start tending to your flame. Building and basking in a secure, self-confident fire within is the secret to your happiness.

2. **Work to make your flame a beacon of welcoming light and warmth**—not a fire hazard. We are so worried about how lovable we are that we don't stop to consider the quality of the love we give.

3. **Stop being a hater.** Instead of player hatin', look, listen, and learn from the flames around you. Bring these admirable qualities out in yourself and watch as your flame gets brighter.

4. **Work on your signature, sensual style** to make your flame exceptional and individual while enhancing your best qualities and letting your perceived flaws go up in smoke.

5. **Stop believing that only certain moths should be attracted to your light.** Don't limit your options with some small-minded list of flame-retardant choices. The moth you turn away because his wings aren't the right color or his cocoon isn't big enough may just be the moth of your dreams. And even if he's not the ultimate moth, he may be there to teach you the lesson that will help draw Mr. Right to your flame.

So I repeat: Be the flame.

FROM THE MOUTHS OF BABES:
WHAT MEN REALLY WANT

Time and time again, men quoted in articles about what they are looking for in a woman say the same thing: they want women who like themselves, who are comfortable and easy to be around, who know what they want sexually, and who appreciate their bodies. In other words, men are drawn to *confident* women who like and value themselves.

> **FROM AN ULTIMATE BABE**
> "Sense of humor is number one for me," George Clooney told *People* magazine in 2006 when asked what he looks for in a woman.

With this in mind, I decided to share some of the interviews I did with several men of different ages, races, economic and marital statuses, asking what attracted them to certain women. I think you'll be as interested as I was to hear their views. Their answers proved to be enlightened and amazingly quite similar. For the record, all the men mentioned, in some form or another, desire that a woman be "attractive" but each had a different idea of what that was. Also, the qualities beyond looks that they mentioned most often were brains, energy, humor, and spirituality.

Be clear, I'm not going through the exercise of what men want so you can change and adjust to their desires, but so you can see that you already possess what men say they want; it simply needs to be fluffed and shared.

1. WHAT ABOUT A PARTICULAR WOMAN WHO WALKS INTO THE ROOM DO YOU FIND ATTRACTIVE, AND WHAT COMMANDS YOUR ATTENTION?

Steve, 45: It's an impression, a vibe. Obvious beauty, of course, is a factor, but I can be moved by the not so obvious, the signals and energy that are given off as she enters the room. **Joe, 59:** For me, sensuality is the spark. I can look at a woman and the way she is groomed, really her attitude toward her dressing, catches my eye. That and mysterious confidence. She'll walk into a room, know she's being checked out, but waits to make eye contact. **Doug, 26:** A woman with a confident demeanor. Someone who's not afraid to get out on the dance floor and have fun, but not a freak either, a lady with a little bit of a wild side. But you get all that from everything about her—walk, talk, dress, who she is with, what drink she orders, how she orders it, etc. You just have to assess well. **Ted, 39:** A soft smile. Her confidence. The way she walks. God-given hair that can be styled in different ways. What she wears and how she wears it. How she innocently but strategically shows off her best attributes. **Matt, 50:** Her style, her energy. It's really about the way a woman carries herself, because style and energy will supersede age and looks.

2. WHAT DO YOU FIND SEXY ABOUT A WOMAN?

Ken, 39: Brains. There is nothing less sexy than striking up a conversation with someone who has no discernible position on why we are in Afghanistan. **Peter, 25:** When she makes me laugh. If a girl is a bit of a goof, it's really hot to me. **Giuseppe, 56:** Passion is what makes a woman sexy. The body may not be perfect, the face more interesting than beautiful, but if a woman has charm, then I want to know her. **David, 32:** A sense of humor and spirituality that matches mine is sexy. **Joe:** Doe eyes, well-manicured hands and feet, subtle imperfections such as a mole on her lower lip or neck. **Matt:** A woman who communicates that she has a sexual appetite and sexual energy in a subtle way that lets you know she's no freak but she's no lady either. **Doug:** When my jaw drops while she is wearing flip-flops, sweatpants, a sports bra, and a hat. Anyone can look good dressed up, but if you can get my attention while you are bumming it—then you must be a keeper. **Steve:** How she carries herself, the kind of signals she sends to me that she's interested, and how she engages with those around her.

3. HOW IMPORTANT IS THE PHYSICAL?

Ken: Physical appearance is very important. I dated several women who I didn't feel were "pretty enough" to show to my friends. Then one day one of my friends was telling me about his new girl and he said, "You're not going to like her—she's not a beauty queen." And then I asked him when was the last time either of us was in the company of a beauty queen, and we both realized that we ought to start worrying more about what we liked about a girl than what our friends liked. **Ted:** Very important. It's what catches the eye and stirs the imagination to wonder. **Steve:** Looks are important but they're part of a dynamic that is complemented by communication. **Joe:** Physical is not important if she knows how to work with what she has. If she's self-conscious about certain physical parts of her body and it shows, that's a turn-off. **Matt:** If she has other things to compensate for the physical—things like wit, intellect, humor, energy, and good conversation, the physical isn't so important, but if she is attractive and has none of the other things, it [the physical] matters even less.

4. WHAT'S THE ONE THING THAT WILL WIN YOU OVER EVERY TIME?

David: If she has matching or complementing qualities that I wish I had. So if I'm at a point in my life that I want to be more organized, and I meet a girl who has her whole life in cute little folders and filing cabinets, wow, that's hot! **Marc, 36:** The way she carries herself—her vibe. And if she is comfortable within her own skin in any environment. **Joe:** Intelligence, wit, sense of humor, and a great smile. **Doug:** Gets me every time—that little smirk from across the room to say "Hello." Even if I have been with a girl for years, that will always make me smile. **Giuseppe:** Eyes that smile at me and tell me what she is really thinking. **Matt:** If she exudes life-force and sexual energy. That tells me she is into life and is a positive person instead of a complainer. I like a little aggressiveness—enough to tell me that she's independent and not trying to sap my energy. **Ted:** The combination of her lips, eyes, and smile. **Vic, 47:** A woman who's loving, generous, honest, and loves to look as beautiful as she feels inside. (And, of course, hot sweaty sex whenever we can get it. LOL!)

Interesting, yes?

HOW GOOD IS YOUR LOVE?

Whenever I give a workshop, I ask the audience, "Who here thinks they are a good lover?" Of course, nearly every woman in the room raises her hand, often with a nervous chuckle, because, hey, who doesn't want to believe that they can drop it like it's hot. But when I ask how many are great lovers *outside* the bedroom, with all their clothes on and various body parts in their proper places, suddenly they're not so sure. Because after all, if they were indeed good lovers, wouldn't they have a man? Wouldn't their marriages feel more intimate? Wouldn't they feel better about themselves in and out of bed?

You know, much of the work of writing a book comes way before you ever sit down to type the words "Once upon a time." The same is true of creating a great love life. Much of the work of being a memorable lover begins way before you ever hit the sheets. And it all begins with your attitude about love.

When it comes to love, too many of us are satisfied simply experiencing love as a state of mind. We allow love to dwell in our hearts and heads, and we fuel this emotion with love songs, poems, and romance novels. We extend our feelings to only those "lovers" we deem acceptable and worthy— spouses, children, parents, siblings, friends—and exclude those who don't fit neatly into our heart-shaped box.

Expand your loving state of mind and make it your quest to exist in a loving state of *being*. Extend the boundaries of your acceptable "lovers" and fill your world, not just your mind, with loving thoughts and actions. A smile, a thought, a good deed toward a stranger is a good way to start. Be a friend instead of a competitor. Accept and return a compliment with a genuine smile. Ask not what your lover can do for you; ask what you can do for your lover.

I truly believe in the quest of falling in love as much as I possibly can. This has meant redefining my idea of what falling in love means. I've expanded my idea from "lifelong partnership" to include any relationship, whether it lasts five minutes, five days, or 50 years, that captures my attention through my heart as well as my head. What I've learned is that it's the short little "love affairs" that keep my heart stimulated and my loving energy constantly engaged.

The only way to receive love is to give it. The only way to be blessed with *quality* love is to offer quality love in return. So just don't crave it, *live* love. Because, ultimately, it's not always about *who* you love, but rather *do* you love.

SEXUAL
WOW

CHAPTER NINE

SED 109-INTRODUCTION TO SEDUCTION

LET YOUR BAD GIRL COME OUT TO PLAY

In a totally unscientific poll conducted on my blog, I posed the question: If you could free your mind, what would you do?

HERE ARE THE RESULTS.

Thirty-seven percent said they'd let their bad girl come out to play.

Nine percent said they'd summon the courage to leave their current relationship.

Twenty percent said they'd leave their job and work their passion.

Thirty-two percent said they'd stop worrying about changing themselves and just be.

Interesting that the majority, 69 percent, said that if they could free their mind of all the rules, expectations, and opinions of others, they would basically live life by their own truth.

Imagine, if you had the strength to do that, how much happier your life would be.

Mind over matter, people. Mind over matter. Or as the saying goes, "If you don't mind, it shouldn't matter."

It was also no surprise that the highest percentage said they'd let their bad girl come out to play. Not a surprise because, among my students and workshop participants, this is by far their number one wish. I can't help thinking about how so many of us good girls are missing out on much of the good clean lust (okay, maybe not squeaky-clean) life has to offer because we're stuck in our good-girl persona.

I say it's time to support the bad girl in you and let her come out to play.

But first, before we do, let's get a few things straight. Being a bad girl *does not mean* being immoral or doing anything illegal; acting cheap or tawdry; disrespecting yourself or others; or engaging in indiscriminate sex. Women who engage in these behaviors aren't bad girls—they are either straight-up confused girls or professionals.

So let's climb out of the lexis trap and define what being bad means for ourselves. Being bad means uncorking and enjoying your sexual energy; it means not squelching your passions but rather giving in to desire; it means loving sex on your own terms, being sexually confident, curious, and spontaneous. It means knowing not only how to give pleasure but how to receive it as well. Being bad means knowing what you want and asking for it, in and out of bed. It means partaking in sensuous loving and being happily orgasmic.

Now, I ask you: Doesn't being bad sound awfully damn good?

So why, then, are we so afraid to explore our sexual sides with the gusto we and our lovers deserve? I know—a loaded question with a history of psychological head trips played on us throughout the generations.

Maybe it's best that we reach back to one of the baddest bad girls of all times for a bit of wisdom. Here is a classic thought from Mae West. Let it be your mantra as you allow your bad girl out to play: "When I'm good, I'm very, very good, but when I'm bad, I'm better."

Free yourself from the boundaries that the expectations of others have placed on you. It's time to *own* your sexuality. It's time to stop being afraid of it and what you think it means to be sexually liberated.

I want to share something that was revealed to me during my meditation session one morning. I asked God to explain to me what his definition of sex was. Whispered in my heart were these words: *Sex is the creative expression of love of self and others.* Powerful, yes? I continued to meditate on that divine definition, breaking it down so I could analyze it more fully. As I interpreted it, anything you could imagine and perform sexually, as long as it was performed and delivered with consent, with respect and love for yourself and your partner, was good.

Now that's a definition of good-girl sex that I can live with! How about you?

So stop settling for "whatever" sex because that's all you think your good girl is entitled to or capable of. If you don't stretch yourself beyond the tight little sexual boundaries most of us live within, you'll never find out how delightfully sexual you really can be.

EXAM

How sexy are you? Take this quick quiz and find out your seduction style.

1. He's raring to go, but you're pooped. You:
a) Go for it! I feel a second wind coming on.
b) Snuggle up, kiss, and caress and see how I feel.
c) Give him a peck goodnight and turn over. I need my rest.

2. Who usually makes the first move?
a) Me
b) 50/50
c) Him

3. What's the sexiest thing one would find in your nightstand drawer?
a) Toys that go buzz in the night.
b) Protection, because safe is sexy.
c) The book I'm currently reading.

4. When it comes to your body, what kind of tour guide are you?
a) I know every main road, back alley, and detour.
b) I am well familiar with the local hot spots.
c) I get lost a lot.

5. He's eager but ineffective. You:

a) Take matters in your own hands and show him exactly how and where you want it.

b) Let him know his effort is sexy, and offer subtle hints about what you want.

c) Say nothing. In time, he'll figure it out.

6. The phone rings and the sexy talk begins. You:

a) Continue—you dialed him!

b) Say the first sexy thing that comes to mind.

c) Hang up on the perv!

7. If you were to introduce something new to your repertoire, it would be:

a) A threesome or something equally hot.

b) The joy of toys.

c) No thanks, I'm good.

8. How important is sex in your life?

a) I could not survive without it.

b) It's very important.

c) Celibacy is not all that bad.

9. What is your coveted lovemaking style?

a) Hot, heavy, wild, and crazy!

b) Passionate and loving.

c) Let's do this so I can get to sleep.

10. Your ideal mate is:
a) The best eye candy around.
b) Loving and romantic.
c) Intelligent.

    Add it up. How many: A's_____ B's_____ C's_____

THE SEDUCTION FACTOR: YOUR SEDUCTION STYLE

SUPER SEDUCTIVE (Mostly A's): You know you're a hot mama and you show it! Energetic and spontaneous, you own your sexual self. You are sexual by nature and enjoy adding spice to your sex life through experimentation. You love to be adventurous and take risks with your partner. You know how to please your lover and yourself, and have no problem communicating your desires. You push the sexual envelope in ways most girls only dream of. As long as you respect yourself and others, your willingness to go there is admirable!

SOLIDLY SEDUCTIVE (Mostly B's): While not as out there as your super-sexy sister, you've got the right attitude about sex and are seductive without going over the top. Sex is a fun and enjoyable experience for you—you revel in your sexual energy and aren't shy about expressing it—but you don't feel the need to force anything. You are confident about yourself and your sexuality, and there is nothing sexier than a girl who is comfortable with who she is.

WAITING TO BE SEDUCED (Mostly C's): Okay, your sex life is teetering on the edge of humdrum. Perhaps you are single or celibate or in a long-term relationship that has fallen into the dreaded sexual rut. Maybe life and its demands have kidnapped your libido. Whatever the reason for your lack of passion, it's time to get back in touch with your sexy side. It is a faulty belief that one must have a partner to celebrate one's sexual self. Don't put your sexy on the shelf just because you're not sexually active. Remember, if you don't use it, you'll lose it—the urge, that is. If you and your partner have fallen into a ditch, more talk, touch, and temptation just might be the remedy.

CHAPTER TEN

WP 110–WOW POWER: BRINGING SEXY BACK
Lesson 1

Welcome to WOW Power: Bringing Sexy Back. The semester is almost over, and if you've been building on each week's lessons, you should be feeling more alive, powerful, and content in your own skin. This week, we begin to take the next steps toward boosting your sexual empowerment by reconnecting your sensual and sexual selves. It's time to take what you've learned and explore your Sexual WOW.

LECTURE: *What is sexy?* To be sexy is the secret wish of the majority of women all over the world. But have you ever really defined sexy—the word, look, and attitude—for yourself, or have you done what most do and let others define it for you? And then, based on this definition, tried in vain to fit into a mental and physical definition that doesn't come close to the reality of your life (not to mention your body)? Out of frustration and a sense of failure, you turn to the books of secrets and techniques that fill the bookshelves, only to find that they might help you get through the night but not through your life. Why? Because most show you the secrets of *acting* like a sex kitten, a red-hot mama, or a bombshell, but they don't show you how to actually *become* one—particularly one who is comfortable and confident in her own skin.

PROFESSOR'S NOTES

There is no cutoff point to being sexy. No age, body shape, weight, height, hair length or bank balance dictates sexy. Why?

Because sexy is as sexy does.

Kindness is sexy. Laughter is sexy. Realness is sexy. Humor is sexy. Bold is sexy. Soft is sexy. Menopause is sexy. *Safe* is sexy. Truth is sexy. Confidence is *way* sexy. Individualism is sexy. Compassion is sexy. Mystery is sexy. Fairness is sexy. Intellect is sexy. Naturalness is sexy. Motherhood is sexy. Celibacy is sexy. Loving God is sexy. Loving yourself is the sexiest!

The truth is that sexy is not uniform. Sexy is an outward expression of your inner feminine confidence. Sexy is an attitude. It's not a style or a cup size. You can't wear someone else's label of who you should be and expect to feel authentic and empowered. And neither is sexy a costume you pull on to play some seductress role. True sexy is *your* sexy—fluffed and shaped in any form you choose.

DAILY FIELD TRIP: On your 20- to 60-minute walk today, take a moment to notice all the different versions of sexy around you. How do men and women, or things (yes, *things* can be sexy—think high heel vs sneaker) stand apart in their attractiveness? Consider what makes them sexy beyond the obvious.

TODAY'S WALKING THOUGHT: *I am the new sexy!*

CLASS ASSIGNMENT: Today is about releasing your sexy attitude for no other reason than because that's who you are. This is not about trying to attract anyone or even pump yourself up to have sex. The goal is to simply be sexy all day because, I'll say it again, *that's who you are*. Interesting assignment, I know. Here are some tips to get you started.

DRESS SEXY TODAY AND EVERY DAY: Don't wait for date night to look like the hot, sensual woman you are, because that's about putting on a costume and not being you. Dressing sexy is not about revealing and inappropriate clothing that draws attention to yourself for all the wrong reasons. It's not about dressing up in all your finest. Dressing sexy is about wearing clothes (in fabrics that feel good on your skin) and sensual signatures that make you feel good about being you. It's outfits that highlight and enhance your most attractive features. Dressing sexy is about your scent, your coiffed hair, your appealing hands and feet. Bottom line: Dressing sexy is about caring about your appearance and making an effort to look good and feel good for *yourself*.

DO THE CLARK KENT. MAKE WHAT'S UNDER THERE INSPIRATIONAL UNDERWEAR. I know I'm back in your underpants, but you can learn a lot from a superhero! No matter what he was wearing on top, underneath Clark was always ready for action. Let your pretty lingerie be your sexy little secret—a secret (always for you, never just for him) that makes you feel attractive and inspires the sexual being in you. So whether it's under a suit, sweats, or jeans, whether you're doing housework or homework, underneath it all wear what makes you feel alluring and sexy.

NOTE-TAKING: Positive, sexy attitudes often get waylaid by negative, hurtful thoughts. Make a list of your top five "terrible toos" (I'm too this, I'm too that). Now make a list of all your attributes that offset those pesky negative thoughts. Recopy this list and display it in your sanctuary.

Beginning this week, each time a terrible too threatens a tantrum, say this to yourself: "I may be too _____, but I'm still way too sexy for me or anyone else who matters to care."

EXERCISE: Continue with three sets of 15 kegels, three times a day. This week, think a sexy thought while you kegel.

Lesson 2

LECTURE: *Sexual energy.* Another potent ingredient of the WOW factor. You know it when you feel it. It's that spark of electricity that makes you stand taller, puts a come-hither glide in your walk, a twinkle in your eye, and a mischievous bend in your smile. It makes you feel happy and eye-catching and invincible. In short, your sexual energy is the announcement of your sensual presence in the world. It charges you up from head to toe and draws all eyes in the room and a few bodies to your side as well. It is a powerful force that attracts you and makes you attractive to others.

But beyond attracting someone, your sexual energy is a potent force in maintaining your health, intimate relationships, and even your spirituality. Sexual energy is passionate and dynamic. It is just as advertised—energy—a passionate, dynamic force.

So if sexual energy is such a profoundly wonderful thing, why do most of us fight so hard to suppress and ignore it? Because for most of our lives, our natural sexual energy has been equated with something wrong or immoral. It frightens the great majority of us, especially married women, because we are supposed to reserve such feelings for our spouses, aren't we? We don't know how to handle our sensual presence when in the company of strangers. When it rears its powerful head, we feel uncomfortable. We do what we've been taught to do: ignore it and let it pass. We're afraid of our sexual energy and where it might take us. Instead of trusting our natural instinct to revel in it, we suppress it because we think if we feel it, we have to act on it.

No, you don't. Trust and appreciate your sexual energy. It

is a God-given gift that is your key to growing your natural sensuality into the power of WOW.

DAILY FIELD TRIP: Enjoy your 20- to 60-minute walk. Today, continue to notice the sexual energy around you.

TODAY'S WALKING THOUGHT: *Feeling sexy feels good!*

CLASS ASSIGNMENT: *Feel and enjoy your sexual energy.* In order to get comfortable with your sexual energy, you first have to understand how you handle yours. So here's a one-question pop quiz: You're at a party and you find yourself sexually attracted to someone else in the room. Do you:

a) Flirt heavily with the intent of getting them into bed?
b) Flirt a little bit and just enjoy how the encounter makes you feel?
c) Suppress your feelings because you're afraid or with someone else?

Your answer will more than likely line up with the results of your Introduction to Seduction exam (A: Super Seductive, B: Solidly Seductive, C: Waiting to be Seduced). If you answered A or C, you're on either end of the uncomfortable scale because you are blocking the sheer pleasure of your sexual energy by feeling the need to *do* something with it. It's okay and important to simply feel and enjoy your sexual energy, without the need to make something happen. If something is going to happen, it will—naturally and without question or hesitation. And if nothing moves it to the next level, you still can feel the empowered pleasure of being sexually viable, and visible, to others.

Bring your sexual energy to the forefront by jump-starting your day with some sexy thoughts, actions, visuals, or words. Try to maintain this level of energy all day. Allow yourself to be fully present in these feelings. Acknowledge and honor any fears, but push through them instead of giving in and ignoring them.

NOTE-TAKING: Journal about your feelings of attraction and particularly the sexual energy you've felt in the presence of someone past or present. Record your negative and positive feelings as well as wishes. How do you treat your sexual energy? Does it give you pleasure, or trip you up and make you feel uncomfortable? If you are married or in a committed relationship, do you think it's wrong to feel sexual energy in the presence of someone other than your lover? Why or why not?

EXERCISE: Continue your three sets of 15 kegels, three times a day. Indulge in a quickie fantasy while you do them.

Lesson 3

LECTURE: *Sex on the brain.* Anyone who knows me knows that one of my favorite sayings is "Where your mind goes, your butt follows." It's clear, concise, and goal-oriented: Action follows thought. This idea applies to everything from making your dreams come true to creating a rip-roaring, passion-filled sex life.

> **I REALIZED THAT...**
> "My great 'aha' moments were those that helped me change my outlook on myself and my participation in my own negative attitude. I now feel responsible for making any change."
> Allison '09

So if you really want to bump up your sex life, it's time to wake up your sexy mind, because once you turn on your brain, the rest of the equipment is sure to rev up as well.

Long-term relationships can put a real damper on your sexy state of mind. In the average relationship, the romantic period when you can't keep sex *off* your mind has an expiration date that comes far too quickly for most of us. The habits you once found endearing become irritating. Combine familiarity with the stress and rush of kids and work, and before you know it, sex has become something else to put on your to-do list. You slip into a state of sexual neutrality— you're rarely in the mood for sex, but you can get there if you have/want/need to.

Long spans of celibacy (whether voluntary or imposed)

forces a similar state upon you. When your brain is no longer continually filled with thoughts of sex and you shut down your sexual energy, you also shut down thinking about yourself as a sensual, sexual being. That's why keeping sex on the brain is so essential to your sexual vitality. Like those Jimmy Choos or those Hershey's Kisses you can't get off your mind—the more you think about something, the more you have to have it. Sex is no different. Wake up that sexy mind and get to know your inner sexiness. We're all so consumed with the condition of our bodies that we're neglecting the biggest turn-on of all.

DAILY FIELD TRIP: Enjoy your daily 20- to 60-minute walk. Think sexy thoughts as you continue to notice the sexual energy around you.

TODAY'S WALKING THOUGHT: *Feeling sexy feels good!*

CLASS ASSIGNMENT: Thinking about sex does not have to interfere with your daily life, but instead will enhance everything about it. A sexy mind generates sexual energy, which makes you feel alive and keeps you ready and wanting to have sex in the wink of an eye, rather than falling victim to predictable, appointment sex. And when your desire is preheated and ready to go, sex stops being something you have to do and starts being something you want to, have to, lucky me, get to do! It also puts your partner on notice that you are a sensual, exciting woman. It puts him where you want him and keeps him there—waiting and wanting *you*.

This week, try one or a combination of these four tips

for reinvigorating your sexy mind. I've gathered them from various sources and have tried them all. They worked for me and for many folks I've recommended them to. I hope they'll help put sex back on your brain too.

1. READ. Studies have shown that women who read romantic fiction have better sex lives than those who don't. My guess is it's because they're exercising their most potent sexual organ—their brain! So read on, and keep an open mind about erotica, which is an entirely different animal than pornography. With something available for every personal taste, erotica can be enjoyable and titillating, and will go a long way toward putting you in a sexy state of mind. (Plus you might just pick up a tip or two.)

PROFESSOR'S NOTES

A word about erotica. I do recommend erotica as a teaching tool, because I firmly believe that many women are drawn to erotica not only for the sex, but also for the way the women in these stories have sex. So when you read erotica, think about your own sex life and compare it, not by *act* but by *attitude*, to those you read about. The characters in erotic stories approach sex in ways that are experimental, curious, adventurous, spontaneous, empowering, and joyful. They are having the kind of sex life real women would love to have. They are pleasing themselves, and by extension, their lovers, without judgment or guilt. That's powerful and very sexy!

Check out *Can't Help the Way That I Feel,* edited by yours truly, and *The I.O.U., The Gift, and The List,* by Elle, from the Elle Series, elegant erotica for the grown and sexy.

2. KEEP THINKING SEXY THOUGHTS. Fantasizing about Idris Elba or Brad Pitt or the guy with the amazing abs you found yourself gazing upon at the gym is not a bad thing. The joy of a pleasurable "mind job" is that you don't have to be responsible or reasonable—or safe, for that matter. Let your mind be a sexy playground where you can fulfill every side of your sexual self—even the freaky side which will probably never see the light of day but can be some serious fuel to keep that lusty fire burning.

3. DO YOURSELF. This may make you a tiny bit (or a lot) uncomfortable, but masturbation can play a big role in keeping sex on the brain. It's a revelation to a lot of women that you don't need a partner to feel sexy and be sexual. Being comfortable with your own body and learning how it works, knowing what turns you on and what doesn't, is essential information for building a good relationship with another person; being comfortable and confident in touching yourself is a huge turn-on to your partner when you're sharing your bed.

4. STAY AWAY FROM NEGATIVE THOUGHTS ABOUT SEX. Parents, pastors, and past experiences may have helped form your opinions about sex, and truth be told, they may not be *your* opinions. Negative ideas, those that seem to fight with your authentic sexual desires, need to be looked at and challenged on the regular. If you don't look at them, you'll continue to believe that "nice girls don't enjoy sex" or "sex is your duty" or "wanting sex makes you a slut." Reprogram your brain to understand that your feminine confidence (that is, your sexual confidence), vitality, and fulfillment are crucial to your existence as a fully alive, fully realized woman. And because your sexual turn-ons are as individual as your fingerprints, who on earth has the right to judge your desires?

NOTE-TAKING: Write down, in detail, some of your sexual fantasies. Don't be bashful or embarrassed. Liberate your desires. They are strictly for your pleasure, so dream away and let them fuel that lusty fire of yours and keep it burning bright.

Explore your feelings about masturbating. How do you feel about the experience and about yourself when you do it? Are you relaxed or nervous? What did you learn about your body and what it likes through masturbation?

EXERCISE: Do three sets of 15 kegels, three times a day. Starting today and every day going forward, use your kegel time to think delicious, yummy, sexy thoughts.

Lesson 4

LECTURE: *Get naked.* When is the last time you were blissfully, brazenly naked just for the heck of it? Not naked because you were about to bathe or get dressed or have sex, but simply because you felt beautiful in the buff?

Nakedness is the epitome of vulnerability. It is, as the cliché goes, letting it all hang out. Often we avoid being naked because we feel our bodies don't measure up to an idealized version of beauty. Or maybe you choose to keep your clothes on because you've been taught that modesty is a good thing—even if you're alone. It appears that between perceived imperfections and stringent moral codes, you are losing out on one of the bare necessities of life—the liberation of body and soul stripped down to your natural beauty.

I REALIZED THAT...
"It's no more old T-shirts to bed!!! It's either silk, body-skimmin', see-through, or nuttin'!!!!"
Dina '08

So the question must be asked: If you aren't comfortable alone in your own naked splendor, how do you expect to feel comfortable and confident in it when in the company of another?

DAILY FIELD TRIP: Enjoy your daily 20- to 60-minute walk. Think sexy thoughts while you stroll, and at least for now, keep your clothes on.

TODAY'S WALKING THOUGHT: *I'm too sexy for my shirt!*

CLASS ASSIGNMENT: *Find time for some naked exploration.* While you're at home alone today, walk around your house (not just your bedroom) naked. Each time you see your reflection, glance at and appreciate the beauty of your body. Take time to admire your most attractive feature and give yourself a compliment before moving on.

Don't immediately towel off and get dressed after your daily shower. Instead, drench your skin with your favorite scented oil and let your body air-dry.

Change your linen and sleep nude on fresh sheets. Before drifting off, think about how wonderful the fabric feels on your naked skin and how sensuous and sexy you feel.

Weather and privacy permitting, go naked outside. Savor the sun's kiss on your naked skin. Dance in the buff and let the breeze brush up against your nipples. Breathe deeply. Take a flower or leaf and gently brush it along the surface of your skin. Focus on the pleasure of touch and the beauty of nature. If there is a private pool or pond you can use, go skinny-dipping and feel the cool water embrace all your body's nooks and crannies.

NOTE-TAKING: What did you learn about your attitudes about nudity? Was today's class assignment easy or difficult for you? If difficult, why? Really probe yourself for the answers to why nudity may make you uncomfortable.

EXERCISE: Indulge in a threesome, or some other outrageous fantasy, as you do your three sets of 15 kegels, three times a day.

Lesson 5

LECTURE: *Own it.* You can feel as sexy as "whoa," dress the role, walk the walk, and talk the talk, but if you don't *own* it, you're still playing a role. Most women, even the divas, don't own it. They flaunt it, work it, use it, and sometimes even abuse it, but they don't own it. Again, *it* is 100 percent feminine confidence in your personal essence, and owning it means living your life without the need for validation or approval from anyone else. A sexy woman who owns *it* is still friendly and approachable, compassionate and considerate, but she isn't about to please anyone before pleasing herself. It's about selfness, not selfishness. It's about understanding your individual truth and making no excuses. If you lease out your feminine confidence, someone can always repossess it. Own it, and it's yours forever.

PROFESSOR'S NOTES

The key to *owning it* is to understand that *being yourself can never be wrong*. This is not to say that you're perfect or that you don't make mistakes or incorrect judgments. It's about realizing that even with all your flaws, you are still fundamentally a strong, beautiful woman just the way you are.

Make an effort to find ways to assert your self-ownership. Start by eliminating the phrase "I'm sorry to bother you, but" and not agreeing to do something that you don't want to do or don't have time to do. Set your own boundaries in all areas of your life.

DAILY FIELD TRIP: Enjoy your daily 20- to 60-minute walk. Fuel your walk with sexual energy and strut as if you *own it.*

TODAY'S WALKING THOUGHT: *I _am_ the new sexy, damn it!*

CLASS ASSIGNMENT: *Resetting your attitude.* Make this weekend a sexy one—one that includes everything *but* sex. (Build up that sexual energy!) This weekend is more about trying out your new attitude and reveling in the positive feelings and attention it brings. It's about stepping out, test-driving and *owning* the unique brand of WOW you've begun to create.

I want you to think about the lessons you've learned this semester, and continue to apply them to this weekend and every day after. Put your sensual signatures together with your charming attitude, and go S.E.L.L. yourself as the confident, sexy, vibrant woman you are to every man, woman, and child you come across. You need not go anywhere special or plan anything special, because true sexy doesn't need a playhouse or audience to exist and be seen. Just be you. Stay in touch with your sensual world; do you and enjoy the feelings of bringing sexy back into your luscious, sensual life.

NOTE-TAKING: Jot down in your journal how you feel about what you learned about yourself this week. Are you enjoying living with your sexual energy? Do you feel sexy? Are you on your way to not only believing that you are a sexy, charming, sensuous woman, but to owning her as well? If not, why not? Who or what do you think is holding her back?

EXERCISE: Three sets of 15 kegels, three times a day. Keep those sexy thoughts coming!

Give yourself a grade based on the amount of work you did this week and how well you applied the lessons learned.

WP 110 CLASS GRADE:

_____

CHAPTER ELEVEN

AOS 111-THE ART OF SEDUCTION
Lesson 1

Well, you've reached the last teaching week of the semester. You've worked on your individual and social sensuality, and bringing your sexy back. Now it's time to take your new sense of feminine confidence and move ahead to the joys and power of sexual WOW, which includes the art of seduction.

LECTURE: *Sexual sensuality.* In the previous unit, we made a very real distinction between teasing and flirting. Now we explore seduction, which is an invitation to your lover, whether subtle or overt, to join you in a completely sensual experience designed to thrill and excite all your senses and culminate in making love.

PROFESSOR'S NOTES

When it comes to the art of seduction, anticipation, excitement, and tension are your keys to turning your man on. Your goal is to create a strong feeling of delicious conflict in him, a conflict which can only be resolved by having you.

Now is the time when all your earlier explorations and discoveries come together to create an authentic, confident sexual being. I hope the work you've been doing has boosted your feminine confidence to an all-time high and you're ready to approach the sexual side of your life with added enthusiasm and assurance.

DAILY FIELD TRIP: Enjoy your daily 20- to 60-minute walk with thoughtful emphasis on the way you move.

TODAY'S WALKING THOUGHT: *Sexy is as sexy does.*

CLASS ASSIGNMENT: *The art of seduction.* Successful seduction is a combination of desire, attitude, and emotion. Trust that the poise that comes from being authentically you will take you far when it comes to moving past flirting and directly into seducing. Think of it as simply taking those S.E.L.L. techniques you've been practicing every day and pushing them in the direction of enticement. Now you will S.E.T. the mood with your smile, eye talk, and touch.

PROFESSOR'S NOTES

A successful seduction occurs when you are able to lure, by any means you see fit, your partner away from whatever unimportant thing he is doing and into your arms. Every relationship—old or new—needs a good seduction every now and again, and the boost it will give your relationship will last for weeks.

Let your mood dictate your actions. Feeling soft and romantic? Seduce him with candlelight and butterfly kisses. Aggressive and in charge? Push him against the wall and take what is yours, girl! The fun and art of seduction is letting all your sexy personalities and moods join in the fun!

SMILE: Smile, but add a twist. Practice your telltale smile that immediately signals to him that you're in the mood. Bottom-lip bite, quick lip lick, whatever it is, save your smile with a twist for when it matters most.

EYE TALK: Look him straight in the eye and tell him everything you are planning to do to his body and what you want him to do to yours. Punctuate it with a twisted smile and watch the smoke start to rise.

TOUCH: Laying on of hands is a huge part of the art of seduction. Gentle arm and thigh brushes and hand caresses are definitely called for with a lover you are familiar with. For a new partner, first touches should be subtle and *almost* accidental. Being playful with a casual, nonsexual touch during the conversation—to make a point, or when he has just made an interesting remark—creates tension and a physical connection. Occasionally touching your own lips or hair, and even running your fingers along the rim or stem of your wineglass, are highly suggestive moves. And more importantly, it sends the message that you're interested in more than small talk.

Make a list of all the qualities, including physical and personality traits, that you think make you seductive. Include those you think are negative. Compare your strengths and weaknesses. Which can be improved on? Which are irrelevant in the big picture and can be tossed? Put together your sensy/sexy tool bag (candles, lingerie, lubricants, toys). Identify a second signature song that turns you on in a sexually suggestive way.

NOTE-TAKING: In your journal, write about your feelings and attitudes about sex and seduction. In your sexual past, how often have you been the seducer versus the seduced? Whose role do you think it is to initiate sex? What has kept you from being more sexually demanding?

Has there been a time in the past when you have seduced a lover? How did you feel about yourself? About him? Did you enjoy being in that role? Did it feel natural, or foreign? Do you feel at this point you've raised your feminine confidence levels to the point of being more aggressive about claiming what you want in the bedroom?

EXERCISE: Practice your seduction S.E.T. while you do three sets of 15 kegels, three times a day.

Lesson 2

LECTURE: *Sex should be fun.* "Laughter and orgasm are great bedfellows," says actor John Callahan, and I concur. When and why did sex become so dang serious? In our quest to boink like porn stars, we've lost one of the great pleasures of intimate sex—fun! Technique, appearance, and the age-old search for multiple orgasms have made sex so goal-oriented and pressure-packed that instead of being the freaks we envision, we've simply freaked ourselves out. Pressure to be the sexual bomb has us faking orgasms and becoming novelty acts instead of authentically sexual, sensual beings.

I REALIZED THAT...
"By becoming more aggressive and playful, I found the young girl buried deep inside—the flirty, playful girl that I used to know."
Marie '07

Fun sex leads to adventurous sex. Share your fantasies; take risks; be creative and shake things up a bit. Fun sex is about learning new tricks and experimenting, and meeting failed experiments (okay, maybe that whole duct tape and lollipop thing wasn't such a great idea) with giggles and kisses, not embarrassment and scorn.

Playful sex also strengthens your intimate ties. Taking away the pressure of performance allows you to feel safer and more secure in your relationship, and this allows you to open up and communicate how you feel and what you want in bed. As time marches on, great intimacy will ultimately trump great sex. And great intimacy is built upon a foundation of loving delight and joy and laughter, not "Ooh, ooh, baby, let me tap that again."

DAILY FIELD TRIP: Enjoy your daily 20- to 60-minute walk fueled by the giggles and memories of fun, sexy times.

TODAY'S WALKING THOUGHT: *Sexy is as sexy does.*

CLASS ASSIGNMENT: Loosen up and start having fun again with sex. Be playful. Great sex should include laughter and joy and not be so serious that you're afraid of making mistakes or not pleasing your lover.

PROFESSOR'S NOTES

Foreplay gives you a new sense of discovery each time you make love. Finding ways to wake up each of your Fan Five prior to actual intercourse increases intimacy as well as pleasure.

With this in mind, begin to prepare for a red-hot night during next week's laboratory. This will be a sexy evening designed to showcase the sensual new you and should entice all your senses. It doesn't matter if you have company or not. A red-hot night can be just as sexy for one as it is for two.

HERE ARE A FEW IDEAS TO THINK ABOUT:

▶ Start with a warm bath or shower drawn in a room treated with candles, fresh rose petals, and scented oils. Don't simply bathe—luxuriate.

▶ Treat yourself to a little decadent dining with a menu featuring favorite finger foods, presented and served in a visually pleasing manner.

▶ After dinner, indulge your senses in good music, wine, and some good loving. If you will be celebrating solo, prepare something new that turns you on.

NOTE-TAKING: In your journal, explore your history of fun sex. Is sex something that has always been sacred and serious for you? How much of a role does laughter and bliss play in your sex life? What about foreplay?

EXERCISE: Continue three sets of 15 kegels, three times a day. Think about the most fun you've ever had while doing the do.

Lesson 3

LECTURE: *Kissing.* Kissing is so important. It's the way we begin our journey into sexuality and it is how we will end our sex lives. It is the most intimate of sex acts, but unfortunately, it is the first thing that gets pushed aside when we discover orgasms and sex becomes more goal-oriented than intimate. Remember, the time will come when your body will lose its ability to be fully sexual, but your lips, those lovely, luscious, sexy lips, will never let you down. Keep kissing. Do it often and do it well. Even now, in your prime sexual years, kissing helps you maintain a playful intimacy and is always the one thing you can say yes to even when your body, exhausted by child-rearing, work, or premenstrual bloating, isn't up for anything more.

PROFESSOR'S NOTES

Did you know that, after the genitals, the lips are the most sensitive part of your body? They are stuffed with nerve endings and can give and receive hours of pleasure. So what's keeping you from puckering up? What are you waiting for? Commence to kissing!

Check out *Seal It with a Kiss: Tips, Tricks, and Techniques for Delivering the Knockout Kiss,* by Violet Blue.

Great kissers know that it's not about the lips or the technique as much as it is about the source of the kiss. An amazing kiss comes from the heart and soul. Your mouth is merely the conduit that delivers the message of your mood, emotions, and intent. An effective kiss really is like a dance—be it a tango, or waltz, or cha-cha-cha—and by moving with the music in your head you are guaranteed to make your lover's head spin!

DAILY FIELD TRIP: Enjoy your daily 20- to 60-minute walk thinking about your first great kiss.

TODAY'S WALKING THOUGHT: *Sexy is as sexy does.*

CLASS ASSIGNMENT: Just as you sign your Jill Hancock to close a deal, your kiss is your lover's signature, the imprint you leave on his lips and his memory. Even if your kisser hasn't been getting the workout it deserves, worry not. You can be up to speed in no time. Just keep in mind the following:

To rediscover or improve your ability to lip-lock with maximum effect, you need to practice hard and often. Start slowly and explore. Hold your own kissing clinic. Announce to your partner that you are in the mood for some serious necking, and take control. Experiment to determine your kissing style. Are you primarily a begin-light-and-end-strong kind of kisser? A lip-bite, tongue-flick kind of girl? A slow, seductive explorer? Or do you simply respond to someone else's kiss? Knowing your basic style allows you to try out pressure and touch and add to your repertoire so you can mix it up. Another great exercise to add to your clinic: Use his mouth and your tongue to instruct him how you like to be kissed elsewhere on your body. This can be quite fun and educational for both of you!

NOTE-TAKING: In your journal, write about your kissing history. Is it something you like, love, don't do? How big a role does kissing play in your romantic life? Why or why not? Rate yourself as a kisser. How did it feel to take control of your kissing situation?

EXERCISE: Continue with three sets of 15 kegels, three times a day. Think about the best kiss you've ever given or received as you kegel.

Lesson 4

LECTURE: *Seduce yourself.* When it comes to sex, too many of us get caught up and bogged down by the expectation that we are supposed to be some sort of irresistible seductress. That it is our job to pump ourselves up just to turn him on. *Not!*

We think that our lovers want to come home to find us wrapped in cellophane, wearing stripper shoes, and swinging from the ceiling fan, all the while purring like a porn star. Not even close. Sure, that might be a fantasy of his, but when it comes right down to it, your mate wants four basic things when it comes to lovemaking:

1. Genuine passion and energy. (There's that word again!)

2. Your *obvious* desire to be there with *him*.

3. That you are confident and comfortable with your body and yourself.

4. To please you.

With this in mind, you can see that walking into the room seduced and turned on is paramount to being a great lover. If you are turned on, he will be too, and it won't matter what you have on or whether your stretch marks are showing.

> ## PROFESSOR'S NOTES
>
> Just as it's hard for some women to graciously accept a compliment, many women don't know how to receive pleasure. They can give and give, but accepting, even when gift-wrapped in toe-tingling love, is difficult for them. You say you want to be an awesome lover? Remember that one of a man's greatest turn-ons is his ability to please his partner. So if you want to be super hot, know when it's time to just sit back and enjoy.

DAILY FIELD TRIP: On your 20- to 60-minute walk today, spend your time thinking of thoughts that get your engine running. Let the visuals around you and your signature sexy song fuel your walking fantasies.

TODAY'S WALKING THOUGHT: *Sexy is as sexy does.*

CLASS ASSIGNMENT: *Dressing for sexual success.* This begins the moment you wake up. Wear your sexiest lingerie beneath your most flattering outfit, and the scent that says "sexy me" with every breath. Feeling good about how you look goes a long way toward self-seduction.

Spend some time putting together what to wear when you want to turn up your social flirting to a teasing and sexual level. (*Now* is the time to think "less is more.") What you wear is up to you, but make sure it's something comfortable and beautiful. Silk or cotton, risqué or demure, it doesn't matter. Whatever turns you on will turn him on. Remember, you're not putting on a costume, but rather a look that represents your signature sexy. Feeling positive and confident about yourself determines how you will give and receive pleasure. Your perceived flaws and performance anxieties will evaporate as your partner responds to a sensually confident you.

Dressing for sexual success demands that everything about you be touchable. Your hair, your skin, and your attire should be inviting to be caressed. Don't forget your mani/pedi, and in the spirit of celebration, paint your nails and lips a flirty, bold new color.

NOTE-TAKING: In your journal, jot down some things that turn you on—or, as I call them, sexy self-starters. Include the small and the large, and be as detailed as possible. Include things about him that float your boat as well. Turn the page and write about how you feel when you are turned on. Do you feel powerful? Adored? Confident? Now think of ways to incorporate your list and that feminine confidence into not only your sex life, but your everyday life as well.

EXERCISE: Continue your three sets of 15 kegels, three times a day. Think outrageous sexy thoughts as you do them.

Lesson 5

LECTURE: *Sensual entertaining.* There are nights when something special and sensually delicious is called for in the romance department. A red-hot night is an amazing way to celebrate Valentine's Day or a birthday or anniversary, but what makes a night like this really hot is when it comes out of the blue for no reason other than to make your lover, or yourself, feel special.

That said, make your RHN more of a celebration about you and your newfound sensuality and sexuality than a quest to "turn your partner out." No need to put that kind of performance anxiety on yourself. Great sex is not about conquest and showmanship. It's about sharing the innermost feminine side of you with whomever you choose.

PROFESSOR'S NOTES

If you are currently without a lover or your relationship has not reached this level, don't think this assignment is not for you. Treat yourself to a sensual evening of self-discovery. Solo sensuality can be a very powerful and telling thing. Knowing yourself sexually is just as important, if not more so, than knowing him. And at the risk of repeating myself, celebrating the lover in you is as worthy and necessary as celebrating the one next to you.

DAILY FIELD TRIP: Today, on your 20- to 60-minute stroll, walk tall, with the thrill of anticipation fueling every step.

TODAY'S WALKING THOUGHT: *Sexy is as sexy does.*

CLASS ASSIGNMENT: Prepare for your red-hot night by doing the RHN Sensuality Questionnaire in the next section. After all, how can you plan for a seductive showcase of your Fantabulous Five if you don't know his sensory preferences?

As you continue planning, here are the rules for successful sensual entertainment.

1. To thine own self be true. At the core of a truly sensual woman is her confidence in her true self. The evening you create should be driven first by your own comfort and enjoyment. Remember the SU number one rule for seduction: Seduce yourself. He is a mere afterthought. I'm not suggesting that you don't incorporate his needs and desires into the evening, but trust me, the pleasure quotient goes up considerably when you enter the room ready to be ravished.

2. Senses rule. Every aspect of your special evening should be planned around your senses. Every sight, sound, smell, taste, and touch should be pleasurable.

3. Anticipation is everything. It heightens your sexual energy and keeps him intrigued. Stay one step ahead. Maintain mystery and you'll surely maintain your lover's interest and gratitude.

4. Be flexible. Anticipation will bring your evening alive. Expectations will kill it. Remember, one of the joys of

living and loving a sensual life is living in the moment and reveling in life as it comes. Plan your evening and then see where it takes you.

5. Drown yourself in pleasure. Not libations or food. You will negate all your hard work and pleasure if you allow yourself or your lover to drink or eat too much.

NOTE-TAKING: In your journal, take a minute to write down your thoughts and anticipations about hosting a red-hot night. What is it that you hope to achieve? What will ultimately make the night a success for you? Afterward, explore how you felt about the evening and your role as the seductress. If you will treat yourself to a sexy and sensual solo evening, write about how you feel about getting in touch with the lover in you sans a partner. What are the main emotions driving your thoughts? If they are mostly negative, explore those feelings and then make a list of all the positive reasons why this is important.

On your red-hot night, give yourself to five star lover treatment. Get up in the morning and put on your sexiest drawers and most flattering outfit. Get your hair done and make sure your makeup is flawless. Feel good about the lover in you all day. That evening, pull out all your treats from your sensual trick bag—the candles, champagne, rose petal bath—and let the one person you tell the least, know that you love her the most. Make special plans for yourself, complete with a gift (jewelry is always a good idea), just as you would the great love of your life. Because after all, aren't you? If not, you should be.

EXERCISE: Continue your three sets of 15 kegels, three times a day. Think outrageous sexy thoughts as you do them.

Give yourself a grade based on the amount of work you did this week and how well you applied the lessons learned.

AOS 111 CLASS GRADE:

_____

RED-HOT NIGHT
SENSUALITY QUESTIONNAIRE

Knowing what turns your senses on is the key to planning a sexually sensuous evening. Take a minute to answer the following questions for yourself and for your partner, and use this information to plan and ignite a red-hot night.

1. My/his favorite color is: _____

_____

2. The fabric I/he like(s) touching my/his body is:_____

_____

3. I/he love(s) the smell of: _____

_____

4. My/his favorite musical instrument is:_____

_____

5. My/his favorite foods are:_____

_____

6. My/his favorite vacation spot is:_____

_____

7. My/his favorite body part of his/mine is:_____

_____

8. My/his sense that is most predominant is:

   a. Sight b. Smell c. Touch d. Taste e. Hearing

CHAPTER TWELVE

SLL 112-SEDUCTIVE LIVING LABORATORY

This week you will put the lessons of the last two weeks into practice and solidify your newfound sense of sexual sensuality. It's going to be a hot, hot week as you turn your lessons into serious lovemaking, even if it's with your sexy self!

LECTURE: Continue to discover your sexual sensibilities. Knowing what turns you on and makes you feel good is the first step in owning your sexual self.

> **PROFESSOR'S NOTES**
> Relax and have fun living seductively this week. Remember that the key to sensual entertaining is being yourself and staying in the moment.

SEXUAL ENERGY: Keeping sex on the brain will go a long way in keeping your sexual energy charged and simmering.

SENSUOUS LOVING: Create memorable experiences together and increase your sexual bliss by incorporating your mood and your Fantabulous Five into to your lovemaking.

SEDUCTION S.E.T.: Practice your S.E.T. techniques (Smile with a twist, bawdy Eye talk, and telling Touch) on yourself so you'll be comfortable and ready when it counts.

CLASS ASSIGNMENT: Red-hot night. Treat yourself or your lover to an intimate night of sensual pleasure.

Take all the lessons you have learned throughout the last three units and incorporate them into a lovely evening of sensuality and sexual discovery. If you are single or your relationship is not yet at this level, don't skimp on planning a sexy solo evening to celebrate the lover in you.

NOTE-TAKING: Take time to record your thoughts and feelings about what you learned this week about yourself through your sexual sensuality.

EXERCISE: Keep kegeling! Three sets of 15 kegels, three times a day. Keep thinking sexy thoughts while you do.

Extra Credit

SEDUCTIVE LIVING LAB MOVIE SUGGESTION

Here's another favorite movie from the SU movie vault. More overtly sexy than the previous suggestions, *Kama Sutra* is still tasteful and beautiful. It is absolutely one of my favorites.

KAMA SUTRA: A TALE OF LOVE. This movie is so sensually hot! Take an Indian prince, his virgin bride, a sensual servant girl, and her forbidden love, combine it with lush, colorful Indian scenery, lessons in the Kama Sutra, and a tear-jerking love story, and you have an amazing tale of love and illicit lust. Tasteful and oh, so *hot! hot! hot!*

The Philosophy of WOW

BE SCANDALOUS!

Oscar Wilde (my ultimate dinner partner) wrote: "One should never make one's debut with a scandal; one should reserve that to give interest to one's old age." Since reading this, I have been intrigued by the idea of being scandalous.

The dictionary defines *scandalous* as "offensive to propriety or morality." *Propriety* is defined as "the quality or state of being proper" and "the standard of what is socially acceptable in conduct and speech."

Wait a high-heeled minute! Just who is the arbitrator of what is socially acceptable? I mean, beyond the Ten Commandments and other generally agreed-upon rules—like no talking to the screen all through a movie, or liberally peppering your speech with *motherf***er* at your child's parent/teacher conference, or using all the toilet paper and not replacing the roll, or sleeping with your best friend's man—who is the wizard behind the curtain? Who is actually in charge of dictating to you and me the nuances of what's socially or morally right?

When I think about the famous women who are sensual and sexual icons, many of them have been considered scandalous in some way. Think of Mae West, Coco Chanel, Marlene Dietrich, Marilyn Monroe, Josephine Baker, Eartha Kitt, Sophia Loren, Elizabeth Taylor, Diana Ross, Cher, Madonna, Angelina Jolie, Jennifer Lopez—all women who by living, working, and loving on their own terms created controversy and concern among the keepers of society's social and moral compass. They didn't live in fear of being judged. Their fear was living without feeling *alive*.

These women lived by their own moral code and rules. While some of their choices led them down rather destructive paths, others achieved great success and happiness; all of them found an authentic life—one that, for good or bad, right or wrong, was dictated by their own sense of individual truth.

The longer I live, the more I become a quiet advocate for living scandalously. Free yourself from other people's opinions about what's right or wrong and do what you have to do to live a life that is full and joyous and satisfying on your terms.

Put a little scandal in your life. It doesn't have to be major what-the-hell-are-you-thinking Lindsay Lohan/Paris Hilton/ Britney Spears crazy-tabloid scandalous. Nobody but you needs to know about it. But do something that excites you; that feels right to you; that is in keeping with your own truth and your own moral code but makes you step outside the boundaries that other people, whether parent or pastor, have placed on you.

Find a place in your life to be a little outrageous. Wear red nail polish or lipstick; unbutton those top three buttons and show a little cleavage; raise your hem two inches; take a skinny-dip; make love on the balcony; take a trip solo and discover something new about yourself; buy a vibrator, or if you have one, share it with your lover; go commando. Take pole dancing lessons or learn to tango. (Did you know that the tango was originally danced in the brothels of poor neighborhoods because it was considered to be scandalous?)

Do something that you don't ordinarily do because other folks think you shouldn't. Follow Oscar Wilde's advice and include a little scandal in your life to give you interest, spice, and memories that bring a sly smile to your lips. Eliminate regret—and failure—from your vocabulary. And if that's not possible, consider the idea that it's better to regret something you *did* than something you *didn't* do.

Scandalous women are sexy. Why? Because passion, confidence, individualism, fearlessness, excitement, curiosity, and a sense of adventure are all prime ingredients of a scandalous personality. And being scandalous doesn't require that you lose your sense of integrity and honesty, just that you lose your fear of being authentically you.

So set your own boundaries, and when in doubt, fall back on these universal truths: Love. Seek joy. Do no harm. Live the truth. Still not sure?

India.Arie said it best: "You know the truth by the way it feels."

SEVEN SIMPLE SEDUCTION
TRICKS AND TREATS

The following flirting/seduction tips are easy and embarrassment-proof. So even if you're still feeling a bit shy about being fast and forward, these suggestions are highly effective but still comfortable. We get so caught up in trying to find the next mind-blowing sex move that we forget it's the simplest things that most often make the sexiest impact.

1. SAY MY NAME

Nicknames can be very endearing, particularly if they are exclusive and packed with sweet sentiments. But sometimes the sexiest and most alluring name of all is his own. If used at the right moment, it packs a wallop of a seductive punch. Say his name at the most intimate moments. Add it to the end of "I love you." Whisper it over and over again in his ear and let him know in no uncertain terms that he is exactly the person you want to be with at this moment. Look him straight in the eye, say his name, and watch the meltdown happen.

2. THINGS LEFT UNSAID

Try this to get your lover's mind racing. This week, every time you see him, smile and think to yourself, *Hey, boy toy, you really have nice lips* (or *You look like sex on a stick,* or whatever it is that turns you on about your BT). It may take him a couple of times to notice, but eventually he will. And when he asks you what you're thinking (and, believe me, it won't take long before he does), say, "Oh, I was just noticing what a nice mouth you have." Smile and go about your business.

While this is an exercise in building your sexual confidence, you're also reminding yourself of the things that initially attracted you to him, plus building anticipation and mystery. As long as you're smiling at him, he's wondering what's going on in a very good way!

3. OLD-SCHOOL SEDUCTION

Remember high school, when you made out on the couch all night? When the lights came on, unfulfilled desire left your legs feeling like jelly and your heart (and other areas south) pounding. And he left hot as hell and full of anticipation for the next time.

The art of delayed gratification has sadly been lost, replaced by our quest for the Big O. What we girls also lost was our sense of empowerment and control over the object of our affection. Take time to practice the art of old-school seduction. This is about affection, sweetness, warmth, romantic kissing, *not* unbridled passion or a prelude to sex.

Reclaim your ability to please and tease. You're setting the stage, making him feel deliciously weak enough to allow you to direct the action, while you build your feminine confidence and perfect your womanly wiles.

4. SPEAK IN CODE

I was watching *The Other Sister*, a movie starring Diane Keaton, in which she used the phrase "olive juice" when she wanted to tell her family "I love you" in a public place or from across the room. I thought, What a great flirt technique. It's special, secret, fun, and endearing. Everything you need to turn your partner on and turn him out!

Get creative and come up with special code words for "I

love you"—or better yet, "I want you"—to use in the most deliciously inappropriate places and times with your spouse or lover. Your code doesn't have to be fancy or particularly poetic, as long as you both know what it means. "My, my, my." "Are strawberries in season?" "I thin I taw a puddy tat." Okay, that last one might make you sound crazy, but you get the point. Finding little ways to help build intimacy and ignite passion will go a long way to keeping your desire for each other alive.

5. TAKE A WALK TOGETHER

Take the object of your desire on a hand-holding stop-every-now-and-again-for-a-kiss   pinch-your-butt-and-bite-your-lip can't-wait-to-get-you-home   eye-message stroll. Join your lover for a flirty walk, preferably in some place bursting with sensory delights; the mall will do just fine, as long as your attention is on him. Snuggle close to his body; hold his hands; talk with your eyes; and make it clear that nobody exists except the two of you. Turn on all your charm in this very public place and you'll push all the right buttons in a most innocent but highly effective manner.

6. SHARE SOME OF YOUR FAVORITE THINGS

I doubt Fräulein Maria had this in mind in *The Sound of Music*, but here's a sexy and very expedient way to share with your lover some of your favorite things, in and out of bed.

Spend a little time jotting down a few of the things that make your heart, head, and other hot spots sing. Include everything from favorite foods and books, clothing, and gift items to sexual treats and techniques. Start innocently and begin to mix in the sex with the other items—yes, make it a definite tease!

This list accomplishes so many things on so many different levels. It's an insight into your playful, sexy personality, a rundown of gifts you'd love to receive and meals you'd love to share, and a seriously sexy "Honey, do" list. Most importantly, it's a great way to communicate your pleasures and preferences.

If your relationship is relatively new, a great time to send this is just before you're intimate for the first time or shortly thereafter. Your favorite things list is a fun and unexpected gesture that will garner you big hottie points. *Always* ask for your partner's list in return. Turnaround in such matters is always fair play! *Never* send your list to his work email. You don't want your favorite things to be the cause of his professional downfall.

7. LET YOUR FINGERS DO THE TALKING

How often do you touch your lover? I'm not talking about in bed or while giving a massage. I'm talking about out-of-the-blue caresses, playing footsie under the dinner table, or holding hands while watching television. Your touch, when it's not called for or expected, is reassuring to the one you love, and it's a great way to convey your heart's message: "You are important to me. I adore you. I like being with you."

These spontaneous touches don't have to lead to anything more, and frankly, they shouldn't, at least not all the time. You don't want to train your partner that every touch leads to sex. But loving touches are the keystone to building the intimacy that will remain and sustain your relationship for the long haul.

SENSUOUS LOVING

Boredom is often cited as a top reason why sex in a long-term relationship fizzles. So, in your attempt to enhance your sexual experience, you begin introducing sex tricks, sex toys, sex talk to your love life. The only problem is that while tricks are great treats to throw into the mix every now and again, they cannot uphold the thrill in the long run because novelty acts never win over the real thing. So don't throw away your toys, but understand that for the long haul, your individual Fantabulous Five can and will provide hours of sensual/sexual bliss in a natural and distinctively personal way.

As you've now realized, living life through your five senses is what puts pleasure in the mundane details that dominate our lives. Sensuous living keeps you grounded in the moment and makes you happier and more appreciative of the world around you. The same is true of sensuous loving. Staying mindful of all that you see, feel, hear, smell, and taste while making love increases your pleasure and keeps your mind and body in the present, thus making you more responsive to your partner. Sensuous loving also helps you create memorable sexual experiences together, rather than simply engaging in sexual acts.

Incorporating anything that stimulates your senses will boost your lovemaking experience to another level. Try different music, textures, locations—things that incorporate your mood and individual preferences *at the time*. Not every lovemaking session need be candlelight and rose petals—though that can be lovely as well. Feeling raw and passionate? Throw on a pumping beat, make love on the sisal rug in the living room, and enjoy the rough, sensual side of your passion.

Feeling cozy and romantic? Make love wrapped in the cool feel of cotton sheets, with the rain as your soundtrack.

Studies show that certain smells like rose, patchouli, and sandalwood increase sexual desire, and having your favorite scents at the ready to ignite with the flick of a match or a quick spritz adds another sensual layer to your lovemaking. But the scents radiating from your partner are perhaps the sexiest of all. Take time to breathe in your lover, from the hint of shampoo left in his hair to his natural body smells.

You can absolutely use food and drink as tools for your lovemaking, but don't feel pressure to make every romp in bed a buffet. You can, however, always have at the ready different flavored breath mints that add sensory variety to your kiss, but be mindful of the variety of natural tastes of your lover's skin and body on your tongue.

Great sex need not always be a major production full of props and preplanning. It really is as simple as being mindful of the sensory stimulation available in your surroundings, tuning in to your present mood, and using your imagination to incorporate these elements into your lovemaking.

STILETTO UNIVERSITY FINAL EXAM

Your lessons are complete. It's time to see how much you've changed. Please take a moment to answer these questions thoughtfully and truthfully based on where you are now in your sensual growth. As always, there are no right or wrong answers.

THE WOMAN:

1. List three words to describe your personality / physical appearance.

a._____   a._____

b._____   b._____

c._____   c._____

2. Since beginning Stiletto University, what has been your most defining moment (positive or negative) as a woman? What is your current perception of yourself?

_____

_____

_____

_____

3. On a scale of 1 to 10, rate your current
   a. Self-esteem _____
   b. Feminine confidence _____
   c. Sexual confidence _____
   d. Social interactions _____

4. Since completing the course, what do you love most now about being you? What do you most dislike?

_____

_____

_____

5. Complete this sentence with the first word that comes to mind: I am _____.

6. A person meeting me for the first time would initially notice my _____.

7. What role does sensuality (defined as living through your five senses) now play in your *everyday* life?

_____

_____

_____

8. Recount your most sensual moment to date since your enrollment at Stiletto U.

_____

_____

_____

9. In what way have you most changed since beginning your SU semester?

_____

_____

_____

10. Have your friends or family noticed a difference in you? If so, how? If you are in a relationship, has he noticed a change? If so, how?

_____

_____

_____

THE CHARMER:

11. List three words to describe yourself as a flirt.

a. _____

b. _____

c. _____

12. I now find it difficult / easy to converse with strangers. (circle one)

13. On a scale of 1 to 10, when it comes to being charming, I'd rate myself as a _____.

14. Since attending SU, what role does sensuality now play in your day-to-day relationship with yourself or your lover?

_____

_____

THE LOVER:

15. On a scale of 1 to 10, how would you rate your *sex* life? _____.

16. Are you now a more sensual / sexual / or accommodating lover? Circle all that apply and add any comments below.

17. Complete this sentence: When it comes to sex, the one thing that has changed about my personality is _____

_____

_____.

18. I have definitely become more _____

_____

_____.

19. What have you learned about yourself as a lover?

_____

_____

_____

_____

20. What role does sensuality now play in your *sex* life?

_____

_____

_____

_____

21. Think about the most rewarding / passionate / exciting sexual experience you've had these past few weeks. Write down what made you feel that way about it and how you felt about yourself during this encounter.

_____

_____

_____

_____

THE STUDENT:

22. Average your class grades to reveal your final Stiletto University grade. If you graded yourself lower than B, what reasons do you think contributed to your lower grade?

_____

_____

_____

_____

23. Did your personal achievements meet your expectations? If so how? If not, why not? Talk about your likes and dislikes, what you learned about yourself, how you and your world have changed, and how solidly sensual you feel.

_____

_____

_____

_____

24. Compare your entrance exam answers to your final exam answers. In which ways have you changed the most? In what areas do you need more work? Repeat those lessons until they become part of your everyday existence.

_____

_____

_____

_____

GRADUATION

STUDENT MIXER

RECONNECT WITH THE STILETTO U ALUMNI FOLLOWING GRADUATION

You met them at the beginning of the semester; now it's time to see what the Stiletto University alumni learned, and how they have been living the Power of WOW since graduation.

SEXY BABY MAMA
—NATASHA

[Note: Numbers in parentheses below are the student's personal ratings at the beginning of the semester.]

Natasha, MSA '07
Home: Connecticut
Age: 32
Married 4 years
8-month-old daughter
Overall Grade: B
Personal Ratings (1–10)
Self-esteem: (7) 8
Feminine Confidence: (4) 6
Sexual Confidence: (4) 8
Social Confidence: (7) 7
Sensual Signatures
Scent: Jasmine
Style: Low-key sophisticated
Symbol: Orchid
Song: "Feeling Good" (Nina Simone)
Charisma: Smart

Moment of Truth: "I saw an old college boyfriend on the train. It was so nice to say hello to him feeling good about myself instead of feeling fat and pitiful!"

Natasha came to Stiletto U searching for post-baby sexy. Our goal was to help her redefine her sexy identity and reestablish a loving, fulfilling sex life based on her new family norm. As a working mom with an infant, Natasha had a hectic schedule, so we highlighted the specific areas where she really wanted to achieve results.

INDIVIDUAL WOW: CHANGING HER ATTITUDE
Natasha needed an attitude shift from "ugly, fat me" to "fabulous work in progress," so she could move forward. Once Natasha stopped mourning her past appearance, her attitudes about her post-baby body began to soften and change. "I threw myself a pity party, and got my share of wallowing in the mud of misery. It actually got boring feeling like that, which was very liberating." We also worked on creating a cost-effective, capsule uniform of well-fitting, basic pieces that complimented her body. Natasha let her signature style accessories be the highlights of this basic canvas while she downsized her body. This helped her feel stylish and sophisticated without wasting money. "Looking better has definitely made me feel better about myself. I don't feel like hiding so much anymore."

SOCIAL WOW: CHARMING HER MISTER
A busy working mother, Natasha knew she was putting her young marriage on the back burner, but didn't have the time nor energy to give her husband the attention he deserved. Our goal was to get Natasha back in touch with the flirty wife she'd shelved to make room for baby. First, she began by clearing the baby clutter from her bedroom and creating a sensual sanctuary for herself and her husband. "Now it feels

nice and fresh and energy is flowing there again." Next, she worked on her EBS, brought on by fatigue and frustration. "I can be really short and impatient with him even though I know he's trying. I've been concentrating more on improving my attitude and flexing my flirting muscles in some way everyday. I'm getting nice vibes in return and I'm enjoying my flirting moments with my sweetheart."

SEXUAL WOW: REDEFINING SEX FOR HER RELATIONSHIP

By defining sex as broader than intercourse, Natasha and her husband stopped letting exhaustion keep them from being intimate and created opportunities to increase the closeness between them. "This took the pressure off and I realized that we could still be sexy and loving together, even when we were both too tired to do it. But the good thing I learned is that I still have a sex drive!!!"

"I've definitely changed. I am calmer and more accepting of myself. I don't feel a sharp sense of dislike about my flaws and faults. In fact, I have a confidence now that they'll be fading away as I embrace my desires for myself. I realize that I'm pretty happy again."

PROFESSOR'S COMMENTS: By semester's end, Natasha was definitely feeling happier and more content with her body image and was "back in the groove." I am proud of her: finding your identity again after childbirth is no joke. The truth, as I see it, is that far too many women don't fight to keep the me in Mommy, and instead give everything to their families, saving nothing for themselves.

The pity party proved to be a great incentive for Natasha

to stop all the woe and whining and move on to the wow and redefining. Sometimes concentrating all your frustration into one weekend of self-serving misery makes you realize just how much time and energy you are wasting on accomplishing absolutely nothing!

Recognizing and acting on a potential issue before it became a problem, was a wise move on Natasha's part. Changing her attitude was key to reinvigorating the romance in her relationship. Natasha and her husband were at first a bit skeptical about redefining sex to include "just" long passionate kisses goodnight, loving, sexy massages, and "active cuddling"—in other words, counting foreplay without intercourse as sex. What they happily learned was that after a week, sometimes two, of cuddle sex, by the time their energy levels and schedules permitted them to have full-on sex, it was explosive and exciting because of all the loving buildup!

WHAT SHE KNOWS NOW: Natasha graduated from SU having learned the important lesson that there would be many image-bending episodes in her life, and letting her physical appearance undermine her view of herself as a confident, sensual woman was a losing strategy and a recipe for disappointment and frustration.

WHERE SHE IS NOW: Unfortunately, Natasha could not be reached for an update.

GOOD GIRLS REALLY CAN BE SEXY TOO
—BRENN

Brenn, MSA '07
Home: Massachusetts
Age: 38
Divorced
14-year-old daughter
Overall Grade: A
Personal Ratings (1–10)
Self-esteem: (10) 10
Feminine Confidence: (3) 10
Sexual Confidence: (2) 8
Social Confidence: (6) 10
Sensual Signatures
Scent: Black Orchid by Tom Ford
Style: Tailored
Symbol: Bamboo
Song: "Crazy Love" (Maxi Priest)
Charisma: Sexy

Moment of Truth: "When my daughter told me that I was so much warmer and cuddly, I knew I was different. That and one of my oldest friends said she noticed that I am no longer 'apologizing' for being me."

What I Want Now: "To savor my experiences and to use what I know to work on not having to validate myself by being the good girl."

Brenn came to Stiletto U feeling "intellectually sexy" and with the hope of beginning to reverse a lifetime of sexual repression and adding sensory pleasure to her life.

Stiletto U was a tough and emotional journey for Brenn. "Sometimes I was scared and unsure, but I am totally happy that I stuck it out, because I now feel solidly sensual."

Here are some of the goals Brenn worked on during her semester.

INDIVIDUAL WOW: SEPARATING HER SENSU-ALITY FROM HER SEXUALITY

Once she was given guidance, Brenn naturally flowed into sensuous living, and she quickly understood the added pleasure it gave to her life. Because it was such an issue, we concentrated on her sense of touch for the entire semester. Each night, Brenn would spend at least 10 minutes moisturizing her body, and record the physical and emotional sensations she experienced. Each week she would focus on a different part of her body, eventually concentrating on her erogenous zones, until she found pleasure instead of terror in her touch. "I've learned to savor and relish the little things. And finally I am able to touch and admire my body without hearing any of the negative things about my physical appearance that I was told as a child."

SOCIAL WOW: EMBRACING HER SOCIAL SENSUALITY

With people she knew, Brenn had no problem socializing, but it was a different story with strangers, particularly men. Brenn attracted a lot of attention, but because she constantly questioned their motives, men were quickly dismissed. By concentrating on smiling and listening, Brenn learned to remain approachable while she got to know people. She was thus able to graciously evaluate their intentions, instead of immediately shutting down for fear of being judged and rejected. This was quite empowering for her. "I talk to people I don't know now. I am accepting that I am attractive and it's okay to be noticed. When men approach me, I am friendly and polite instead of my former self, cold and dismissive." Determining her personal charisma was a key turning point for Brenn. "I kept telling myself that I belonged in the Smart Charisma but acted like more of a Cool Charisma. I did this for two days, but it still didn't resonate. I was bawling by the time I admitted that I was really a Sexy Charisma and had suppressed it in every possible way."

SEXUAL WOW: ACCEPTING HER SEXUAL SENSUALITY

Brenn began dating a man while enrolled in Stiletto U. This was helpful, as she could put her weekly class assignments and homework into action. She accessed her inner diva, Tasha. By stepping outside Brenn and letting Tasha take control, Brenn became bolder and more confident, and empowered herself by bringing into balance the sexy side of her identity she'd always denied and kept hidden. "Sex is still a work in progress, but I have definitely changed here as well. I had this amazing kissing session. I felt confident and in charge and really there, experiencing it all. All I intended and wanted was to kiss him, and that's all I did. The old me would have had bad sex out of my warped sense of obligation."

"I gave myself an A as my overall grade because I worked

my butt off! But Stiletto U exceeded my expectations. I feel so completely in touch with my sensual side. I feel lighter. I touch more and am learning to laugh instead of merely showing my teeth."

On her final exam, the woman who described herself as wearing a size 10 shoe now describes herself as "sexy, sexy, sexy." She says, "I had almost become my grandmother, and adopted her values. The me that most people saw was really her. Now I would like to just be me, in every thought, decision, and action."

PROFESSOR'S COMMENTS: I am so proud of Brenn because she put a lot of work into her SU assignments, and as a result, made astounding progress. She had to face a lot of demons, and she did so with grace and valor. Words are important to Brenn as an intellectual, and pulling her out of the lexis trap proved to be hard, but beneficial. The words *savor* and *scandalous* particularly resonated with her, and she was able to take them, define them for herself, and use them as affirming mantras and cues to particular ways of thinking or acting. Defining and using her inner diva, Tasha, to help her through difficult social situations also proved to be a huge help in moving Brenn forward toward her more sexually confident self.

WHAT SHE KNOWS NOW: The most important lesson Brenn learned, and is now trying to master, is that attempting to live her life through other people's rules and expectations is frustrating at best, and crippling at worst. By discovering her true self and individual truth—that she could be smart *and* sexy, and that sex is a God-given gift and she its lucky recipient—Brenn was able to put aside her grandmother's moral values and determine her own moral boundaries to live and love by.

WHERE SHE IS NOW: Brenn was still single and working on her sexual confidence when her semester ended. As we went to print, she had just ended a year long relationship. Brenn admits that the breakup did set her back and led to a sizable depression. "The sensuality lessons were instrumental in my recovery. I slept with the Stiletto U binder next to me for two weeks and would randomly read it when I couldn't sleep. When I began to chastise myself, I read through it. That voice, my inner critic, is slowly fading."

And while her relationship ended, a much stronger Brenn emerged to share her revelations. "It took him and the recent events to help me realize that I really, truly just want to be loved, warmly and fuzzily, that the love should come naturally and not require my talking myself into it. I get it now—you have to own the love you need. I know, now, how I want to love and be loved."

SEXY AND NO LONGER ALONE
—VIRGINIA

Virginia, MSA '07
Home: New Jersey
Age: 42
Divorced
Overall Grade: B
Personal Ratings (1–10)
Self-esteem: (8) 10+
Feminine Confidence: (7) 10+
Sexual Confidence: (6) 10+
Social Confidence: (7) 10+
Sensual Signatures
Scent: Nude by Bill Blass
Style: Fashionably chic
Symbol: The color green
Song: "Golden" (Jill Scott)
Charisma: Cute

Moment of Truth: "When I realized that I'm living the 'I am ...' That I believed that I was fabulous, just the way I am. That is freedom."

What I Want Now: "To work on the healthier 'I am ...' I want to lose weight and find, as Oprah says, a career that I love so much I'd do it for free!"

Virginia came to Stiletto U feeling that she had everything she needed to meet the right kind of guy, but she was having no luck and her confidence was slipping away.

"SU helped me figure out who I really was, not just who I thought I was. Now I live outwardly what I feel inwardly. What I ultimately learned was how to express myself and make the most out of my life, instead of waiting for a man to acknowledge me so I could start living."

Touching base with who Virginia was beyond the surface charm was our main goal. Here are the highlights from her SU units.

INDIVIDUAL WOW: SYNCHRONIZING HER INNER AND OUTER SELVES

"I loved putting together my sensual signatures because they forced me to look at myself as a total package. When my co-workers started noticing my increased sensuality, I realized that I was finally letting the world see what I have always been feeling inside."

A big "aha" moment came through one of the note-taking exercises, when Virginia realized that she'd been portraying the image of a chameleon, changing and adapting to the likes and dislikes of her partners. "I was seeking approval from whomever as long as it validated me. I'd taken bits and pieces from each failed relationship and was sending out vibes that were not the real me. I needed to find the real me."

Virginia's soul-searching during this unit brought startling revelations about how she perceived herself, and about her sorry dating record. "Yes, I knew how to be charming and aggressive, but could I hold a man's attention or he hold mine? I realized that I saw myself as boring. I could speak to anyone about my work, but when it came to meeting men, I had nothing really interesting to say after the initial flirting."

SOCIAL WOW: GOING DEEPER THAN INITIAL FLIRTATION

Virginia also worked hard to identify and investigate her passions outside of work. The more she pursued her own interests, the more interesting she became to herself and others around her. Finding her true self became a huge turning point in her ability to take her charm beyond the surface. "My perception of myself has improved tremendously! I've had a variety of conversations with men I didn't even realize were interested in me, regarding other things besides work. I don't feel boring or like I have nothing of importance to say.

"I realized that I'd spent most of my time talking and thinking about my failed relationships rather than myself and my own journey. This was a huge hurdle for me to jump, but now I feel that I am finally in control of my future.

"I've always been a social butterfly but now I am much more assertive in the way that I approach life. I'm more open to possibilities and am not focusing so much on the limitations that may arise. My co-workers notice that I am more open and I look for more opportunities to be out and engaged in life."

While socially comfortable, Virginia had to work hard to become more assertive and open when it came to men. The more confident she became in her true self, the more comfortable she felt being in control of her dating life. "We made up this acronym—KTP, Keep the Power. It reminded me that I was not waiting for any man to judge or determine if he wanted to be with me, but I was the one with the power to decide that for myself. It worked!"

SEXUAL WOW: BEING SEXY ALL THE TIME

As Virginia's feminine confidence began to gel into the real thing based on who she truly was at her core, she found a new surge in her sexual confidence as well. "I thought that good sex was a big mystery and something I couldn't fulfill, but now I'm not so bound up by my hang-ups over sex. I've learned to ask and get what I want.

"Before Stiletto U, I always felt I had to put my sexuality away until I had a man to share it with. Now it's just a part of who I am all the time, no matter what.

"During the past thirty days, I have fallen in love with myself and with life. Now I want to live life to the fullest and plan for the future I want to have. I was holding me back with negative thinking. I can do all that and still be a lady when I want to be, a sexy lover when I choose to be, and confident being both."

PROFESSOR'S COMMENTS: Virginia came to Stiletto U with a high sense of self and a very positive attitude. She was definitely more charming than most, but it was more of a surface application than a trueness within. By getting in touch with her sensual core, she began to feel more able to define what she really wanted out of her life and a relationship. The positive reinforcement from her friends and co-workers only served to boost her confidence on all levels, including her sexual confidence. By the end of our semester, Virginia had begun dating a new man whom she met online.

WHAT SHE NOW KNOWS: By going beyond the surface and getting to know her true self, Virginia realized that she hadn't been attracting the kind of man she sought, because she didn't understand what she really wanted from herself. She'd been waiting for a relationship to fill the gaps in her personal journey, not understanding that her incomplete energy was attracting more of the same. In the past, when relationships hadn't worked out, she thought something was wrong with *them*. She has now come to realize that by working to become the best woman and lover she could be, she would eventually attract the same.

WHERE SHE IS NOW: After earning her MSA from Stiletto University, Virginia went back to school and got her masters in psychology. She is still embracing the sensual lifestyle. "It helps clear my head and keeps me feeling positive about nearly everything." The relationship Virginia had begun during her SU semester ended on a mutually agreeable note. "For the first time, I didn't feel rejected. In fact, I've never felt this good about a break-up before." As we went to print, she and her new boyfriend of over a year are going strong. "I am happy and in love and finally having the best sex of my entire life!"

TAKING BACK MY SEXY
—ANTOINETTE

Antoinette, MSA '08
Home: Florida
Age: 52
Married 8 years
3 children under 12
Overall Grade: B
Personal Ratings (1–10)
Self-esteem: (6) 9
Feminine Confidence: (6) 8
Sexual Confidence: (4) 7
Social Confidence: (7) 9
Sensual Signatures
Scent: Christmas
Style: Laid-back funky
Symbol: Moon
Song: "Brick House" (Commodores)
Charisma: Cool

Moment of Truth: "When I realized that if I put my mind to it, I could lift my mood by changing the way I looked at things."

What I Want Now: "To keep taking the initiative when it comes to sex and when it comes to everything else, just go along for the ride."

When she came to SU, Antoinette, married to a man 12 years her junior, was two years into the aftermath of her husband's affair, which had rocked her self-esteem and crushed her sexual confidence. Upon her arrival at SU, she thought of herself as modest and voluptuous. By the time her final exam rolled around, she thought of herself as happy and sexy. "I love that I'm no longer feeling so closed off sexually. Feeling happy has made me feel attractive and appealing again."

Taking her broken pieces and creating a whole was our main goal for Antoinette's semester. Here are some of the highlights.

INDIVIDUAL WOW: REDISCOVERING HER SENSUOUS SIDE

Antoinette's innate vibrancy had gotten lost under the stress of motherhood and a broken marriage. To get back in touch with her sensual world, she started reexploring it with her children by mindfully incorporating sensuality into their daily routine. "I really enjoyed this. The kids and I had a chance to hang out more and it made their regular chores more fun. Also, doing it like this didn't encroach on our already busy schedule. I reopened my eyes to the world, kind of like seeing Christmas again through the eyes of the kids. I feel happier more often now."

Creating her sensual signatures started in Antoinette's closet. "Before I became a full-time stepmom, I'd always thought of myself as stylish, but kids really do make you look at yourself differently. I was now somebody's mom and I felt the need to dress accordingly. Plus, having three kids and a job doesn't leave you a lot of time to worry about being fashion forward, but comfortable and clean don't equal fun and sexy.

"Looking at all my old clothes, I realized I had morphed into a mom and stopped being a woman. Creating my signature look helped me find Antoinette among all the different women I play each day."

SOCIAL WOW: REGAINING HER BUTTERFLY WINGS

Her husband's infidelity had totally crushed Antoinette's feminine and sexual confidence. She was feeling like the old lady for the first time in their relationship and was unsure if he still found her appealing. Antoinette found that learning and using the S.E.L.L. techniques was helpful in building up her feminine confidence both in and outside her home.

"For my midterm exam, I decided to go out by myself to a cocktail party at a business conference I was attending. I wore my favorite dress and heels, and me and my inner diva went downstairs. I took the list of cocktails and ordered a Green Tea martini. It was a real conversation starter. This very successful, attractive man came over to me and was openly flirting with me, and I flirted back. It felt great to open myself up to the attention of other men. Not in a 'Come sleep with me' way, but in a fun, friendly way. I went home feeling good about myself. Something clicked inside me and I felt like my sexy light had gone back on. I felt like I had some of my power back."

During her midterm, Antoinette was reminded that keeping her charming self open and available didn't mean that she was looking to be picked up, only that she enjoyed being curious and picking other people's brains. "It was good to know that I could still hold an interesting conversation and that other men find me attractive."

Taking that knowledge about herself home with her, Antoinette felt her feminine confidence begin to bloom again and felt that her sense of sexual relevancy, despite her age and body shape, was alive and well.

SEXUAL WOW: TAKING HER SEXY BACK

It is well documented that when it comes to sex, men are visually stimulated and women are more mentally turned on. So when her trust was broken by the man she loved, Antoinette's head was no longer in the game. Her sex life with her husband had gone downhill considerably since his confession, both in frequency and quality, and Antoinette was unsure how to get her sexy back. "He was much more experienced than me, and my feelings of inadequacy only intensified after the affair."

It was important for Antoinette to get in touch with her bad girl and break out of the modest mom role she'd been living. She decided to combine physical exercise with a stretching of her comfort zone and signed up for pole dancing. "I loved it! I never felt so sexy in my body."

It was also vital that she sexually empower herself and restart her sex life on her own terms. But before doing so, she had to make two attitude readjustments. First, she needed to view her husband again without all the baggage by making a concerted effort to see the qualities about him that she fell in love with in the first place. "I took a positive survey and did regain more of an appreciation for him and the fun we used to have." Next, Antoinette (along with her inner diva) took her S.E.L.L. techniques and applied them to her mate, which helped her acquire a second new mind-set: her husband as boy toy. This change of attitude helped build her confidence as a sexual being while creating a sense of mystery and anticipation for both of them. "I really loved the eye talking because I could say in my mind things I'd never say out loud, and that made me feel really sexy and powerful. And feeling that way made me act that way. He loved it and so did I.

"I thought my husband could read my mind and should know what I wanted or didn't want. Now I realize that he can't, and he shouldn't, because if he can, it means that I'm staying the same and being predictable.

"This was an amazing experience for me. I feel empowered—I'm a grown and changed woman. I never want to be in that place again, and even though I'm not fully where I want to be, I am working to get there!"

PROFESSOR'S COMMENTS: Women who use all their womanly wiles to land the men of their dreams too often turn them off as soon as they put a ring on. Antoinette learned the hard way that shutting off her charm and sexual energy to the world inevitably led to shutting it down at home as well, which led to a multitude of unsavory feelings of frustration and rejection. Antoinette had allowed the balance of power between herself and her husband to shift to his side, giving him the ability to shut down her confidence and make her question her sexual relevance.

WHAT SHE KNOWS NOW: Antoinette learned that the only person capable of stripping away her sexual relevancy and feelings of sexual vibrancy is herself, and that her passion, just like her happiness, is not something that anyone else can create for her.

WHERE SHE IS NOW: Two years after completing her Stiletto University semester, Antoinette filed for divorce from her husband. "I really tried, but I realized that I was trying to save a marriage that no longer worked. Not only was the trust gone, but I was a different woman. Stiletto U really helped me sort out who I was and what I wanted. The first year was depressing, but now we've all adjusted to the new family dynamic, and I'm in a steady relationship with a wonderful man with whom I feel really good being myself. I definitely feel sexy again and I'm having a wonderful time!"

THE TRUTH IS SO MUCH SEXIER
—DINA

Dina, MSA '08
Home: Michigan
Age: 35
Married 7 years
4-year-old twins
Overall Grade: A+/C-
Personal Ratings (1–10)
Self-esteem: (7) 8
Feminine Confidence: (4) 9
Sexual Confidence: (4) 6
Social Confidence: (7) 9
Sensual Signatures
Scent: Echo
Style: Comfort/funky
Symbol: Butterfly
Song: "Golden" (Jill Scott)
Charisma: Smart/humorous

Moment of Truth: "*I am woman!* No, really.
I really believe that I am just more attractive.
Not prettier. The inner happiness that I have is now
apparent on my face."

What I Want Now: "For this to be totally innate
without feeling any guilt about being selfish for taking
time for myself."

Dina came to Stiletto University feeling "smart and funny." She graduated feeling sensual, sexy, and courageous enough to reveal to her husband secrets she'd been keeping for years.

Stiletto U became an eye-opening adventure for Dina, one she shared step by step with her husband and a few friends, which made the experience, though hard work, much more fun. As shocked and pleased as they were with her many changes, nobody was more surprised than Dina herself.

"I now see myself as sexy, smart and powerful. I've discovered my own innate femininity. My friends and family have absolutely noticed the change in me. I've actually been the victim of some 'hateration!' One night, we all went to a party and I was talking with a guy I'd never met before. My girlfriend came across the room, sat down between us, and started talking to him. I could tell the guy was like, What the hell? but I just got into a conversation with someone else. Later she told me that I already had a man and shouldn't be hogging all the attention. LOLLL! Me, the eternal wallflower! I could really tell she wasn't used to the 'new' me."

Here are some of the highlights from Dina's semester.

INDIVIDUAL WOW: TAKING HERSELF SERIOUSLY AS A WOMAN

This woman, whose attempt at being sensual when she started at Stiletto U was "Try not to be too musty at the end of the day," was regularly indulging her love of spa treatments by the time she graduated. "I'm not a construction worker; I'm a woman, damn it! Now I make a much more conscious effort to make my surroundings pleasing to my eyes, ears, nose, and fingers." Most importantly, Dina learned a valuable lesson that every woman, especially mothers, should practice regularly: put yourself on the list of people you take care of. "I have put myself higher on my priority list. If my hubby is running low on prime cuts of meat for dinner, but I need money to buy another bottle of my signature scent, guess who's eating meatloaf!"

SOCIAL WOW: MIXING HER FUNNY WITH FEMININE CHARM

Dina always found it easy to converse with strangers, but since completing Stiletto U she's engaging people on an entirely different level. "Before, it was easy for me to make someone laugh. Now it's easy because I'm genuinely interested." While she once thought that flirting was a great way "to get free stuff," Dina now understands the power that comes with benevolent charm. "Being socially competent on this level is very empowering. I can change a person's attitude."

SEXUAL WOW: HONORING HER DESIRES AND THE TRUTH

This unit provided the most anxiety for Dina. After successfully completing the previous two units, her feminine and social confidence were running high, but now she had to confront her sex life and reveal to her husband that she'd been faking her sexual enjoyment and orgasms for years. From her lack of orgasm to feeling "kissing handicapped," she needed to come clean, because she was cheating herself and her husband. Dina decided to include him as her "lab partner" and asked for his assistance in bringing out her sexy side, letting him know that he would have to endure some experimental kissing, touching, and sexual techniques.

As we both suspected, he was happy to be supportive!

Each week, Dina and her husband worked on one aspect of their sex life. Taking the lead, she would experiment with various kisses, learning how she liked to kiss, and in turn teaching him how to kiss her. The same went for touching and caressing, and making love. The result was a huge increase in intimacy, passion, and pleasure between them, and an increase in Dina's sexual confidence.

"I touch my hubby in passing more or just kiss him for no reason. I am aware of his senses and try to respond in a way that is pleasing to him. He has never been as interested and loves the change in me. He always wanted me to feel good about myself. The kissing is *much* better and I am definitely not as anxious about sex. We're still working on the orgasm part, but it's okay. It feels better and more honest now that he knows the truth.

"I gave myself an A plus as my overall grade because I worked my butt off, and a C minus because I know that this process in the bedroom will take time. My hubby's ego is bruised, but I feel I at least have a starting point to repair some of the damage I've allowed to happen."

On her final exam, the woman who had earlier described herself as overweight and bookish now described herself as "attractive and classy," and she went from being just an accommodating lover to being a sensual one. "I didn't realize how much I was thinking about everything but sex when I was having sex. Because I'm more in the present, I've become more responsive.

"I'm so much happier now. I'm not invisible anymore. I'm letting myself be seen."

PROFESSOR'S COMMENTS: Dina was fun to work with because she was so dang funny, but lurking behind her self-disparaging jokes was real pain. Like most of us, she wanted to feel and look sexy, but because she didn't fit the celebrity or advertising mold, she was convinced that being the wallflower and clown was her fate and didn't even try. Dina donned an attitude of "If I can't be sexy, I can still be smart" and stopped caring about her femininity and sexual self—because if she didn't care, other people wouldn't either. But she did care, and through her work at SU she unearthed a fabulous gem of a woman who is funny, smart, compassionate, and sexy as hell. When her perception about herself changed, so did the perceptions of those around her. What Dina was ultimately looking for was someone to give her permission to be herself. Through her work at SU, she realized that the only person who could do that was Dina, and once she learned that lesson, everything changed.

WHAT SHE KNOWS NOW: Hiding behind any personal strength, in Dina's case her intelligence and humor, can often become a weakness detrimental to balanced, personal growth. She no longer has to fall back on her brain or jokes to deflect her insecurities or get noticed. She's now feeling more centered and letting all her inner and outer beauty shine. Most importantly, Dina knows now that honestly communicating her needs, and asking her hubby to communicate his, was the most intimate and sexy boost she could give her marriage.

WHERE SHE IS NOW: "I am so happy! The biggest gift I gave myself since graduating from SU is giving myself permission to live the way I want without caring what other people think. Now I feel I am truly the woman that God intended me to be. I feel beautiful, interesting, and passionate about my family and my life. My marriage is so much better. I went from simply consenting to have sex to thinking about it all the time like a sixteen-year-old boy! My husband and I are talking, touching, and kissing more, and I don't have to fake orgasms anymore! Yippee!!"

TOO FLY NOT TO BE SEXY
—JANINE

Janine, MSA '08
Home: Pennsylvania
Age: 25
Single
Overall Grade: B+
Personal Ratings (1–10)
Self-esteem: (6) 8
Feminine Confidence: (6) 8
Sexual Confidence: (6) 8
Social Confidence: (5) 8
Sensual Signatures
Scent: L.A.M.B. by Gwen Stefani
Style: Girly glam
Symbol: Star
Song: "Whatever Lola Wants" (Sarah Vaughan)
Charisma: Cool

Moment of Truth: "When I was told, 'You can't be that woman if you can't handle that woman.' Those words allowed me to put both my fears and past experiences into context."

What I Want Now: "Good health so I can continue to pursue the life I was meant to live."

Janine, the young woman who entered Stiletto U calling herself shy, quiet, and loyal, left our virtual halls feeling charming, outgoing, and happy.

"I didn't realize how much of a box I was in until I stepped outside. Now I feel like I'm coming into my own. I love myself for being more daring and opening up to new adventures and opportunities."

At 25, Janine, a beautiful girl by anyone's standards, was understandably still in search of herself. Her crippling shyness and insecurities were keeping her cocooned within a safe but stagnant lifestyle and holding her back from exploring the world and her life to the fullest. Our main goal for Janine was to help her find the budding woman, designer, and lover within, and to build up her confidence enough to share them with the world.

Here are the highlights from Janine's semester at SU.

INDIVIDUAL WOW: DISCOVERING HERSELF WITHIN HER SENSUAL WORLD

Getting in touch with her sensual world was a major revelation for Janine. "At first it was like I never had my eyes open before! Being more aware of my surroundings made me take pleasure in my everyday life. My favorite color is green, and I swear I never noticed how many shades there were in the trees before! Now I realize that slowing down does make life more enjoyable. I'm thinking about my sensuality less and doing it more.

"But it changed me too. I'm more relaxed and even have a better attitude at work. I just feel happier in general. Things that used to bother me don't anymore. I have the choice to be grumpy or not. I decide not."

SOCIAL WOW: FROM CATERPILLAR TO SOCIAL BUTTERFLY

Janine arrived at Stiletto U with real trust issues, positive that at the tender age of 25 she had all the friends she needed. "I never had girlfriends over to my apartment before. I didn't like opening myself to being judged in any way. But now I'm not so afraid of being rejected, so I've stopped putting my guard up."

The woman who usually ate lunch by herself in her office was now eating in the company cafeteria and meeting new people. "It feels good to be more social. My co-workers have noticed a real difference. Before, they never knew what to expect from me, but now we have real conversations. People are a lot more friendly to me now, because of the smiling—it's so powerful."

Through her SU work, Janine began to let her true self shine, and the positive feedback she received fueled her confidence, prompting her to step further outside her comfort zone.

"I went to New York to an art exhibit by myself. I've never gone anywhere alone before—I always went places with a friend. It felt so good to be bold like that. I felt so comfortable. I actually got lost and wasn't upset about it because I was enjoying myself and taking in everything. I would never have done that before.

"I even made a new friend on the train. It felt good to open myself up. Normally I would have sat by myself and texted someone; instead, we talked, and we clicked."

SEXUAL WOW: TURNING SOCIAL CONFI-DENCE INTO SEXUAL CONFIDENCE

Once Janine felt empowered in other areas of her life, bringing that confidence into the bedroom was her next goal. Janine's relationship with sex was young and unfortunately tainted by a domineering first lover. The first thing we did was help her recycle her hurt and anger from her previous relationship into forgiveness and acceptance of herself and her new boyfriend. "I'm learning to block out all the negative voices and concentrate on who I am now."

Youth and inexperience can be a scary combination when it comes to sex. On her entrance exam, Janine stated that she wanted to release her "inner sex kitten." Instead, we helped her release her true sexy self.

"When I came to Stiletto U, I felt that sex was an obligation and something that happened to me. I didn't feel I was contributing very much. And a big part of me was scared and ashamed to claim my desires. Now, with the added sensuality and confidence, I feel so much more powerful in my relationship. And I don't feel that I have to know everything. It's more like, Whatever happens, happens—but in a good way, because now I'm doing my part and we're both having fun.

"I realized that I was creating so much stress for myself. Changing my attitude made my life so much easier. Petty things don't bother me anymore. My overall grade was a B plus, and I gave myself eights across the board because that's my new starting point. I've changed so much that it feels like a ten, but I know I still have room for improvement."

PROFESSOR'S COMMENTS: We really unleashed the genie this time! Janine is definitely a more confident, vibrant young woman. Her confidence levels are through the roof. The woman who didn't need any more friends is now traveling to New York by herself and making lunch dates with new acquaintances. The woman who was so afraid of failing that she didn't try college has opened a bank account to save for tuition and is making concrete plans for her future. I loved working with Janine because, as any woman who's made it past her thirties knows, the twenties can be hell on your feminine confidence. Helping her unearth her self-esteem and see the woman she is becoming at this tender age will go a long way in improving her life and self-image as she grows into full-fledged womanhood.

WHAT SHE KNOWS NOW: Janine learned that hiding your light for fear of rejection takes a huge toll on the quality of your life and personal growth, and that rejecting others before they can reject you is a classic from the "Way to end up unhappy and alone" playbook. By taking chances and letting people see who she is, Janine is well on the road to becoming who she wants to be.

WHERE SHE IS NOW: Janine is pursuing her dream of becoming a graphic artist and is currently enrolled in design classes. "I'd put my dream on hold for so long. By opening up and sharing it with others it became more real, and their encouragement helped me move forward." She is currently single but says she is "finally feeling like I'm being me, and that there is a whole world out there waiting for me to discover."

SEXY AT ANY WEIGHT
—CATHY

Cathy, MSA '09
Home: Georgia
Age: 46
Single
Overall Grade: A-
Personal Ratings (1–10)
Self-esteem: (6) 8
Feminine Confidence: (2) 9
Sexual Confidence: (2) 2
Social Confidence: (6) 8
Sensual Signatures
Scent: Vanilla
Style: Comfortable casual
Symbol: Diamond
Song: "I'm Every Woman" (Whitney Houston)
Charisma: Power

Moment of Truth: "Realizing the power of a smile.
People are smiling back and I feel more confident
because I am not being rejected!"

What I Want Now: "To continue living and see what's
out there."

On her final exam, when asked to describe herself as a flirt, Cathy, the woman who didn't know what it meant to be womanly, replied with three words: I. Am. Able.

"How have I changed? Let's see, I smile more, take time to consider what to wear. I am friendlier, more positive, feel better, and I learned that my sensuality adds another interesting layer to me. I'm pleased by the woman I am becoming."

Here are some of the highlights from Cathy's semester.

INDIVIDUAL WOW: DEFINING FEMININITY

Giving Cathy permission to define for herself what it meant to be a woman moved her from feeling like an outsider in the feminine sisterhood to feeling like one of the girls, but on her own terms. "Since completing the course, the thing I love most about me is that I can smile and be more girly and not be afraid of looking weak. I now live, breathe, and exude my femininity. The biggest thing is that I started caring again. I wasted so much time hiding and pretending that I didn't.

"I'm taking time to think about what I'm wearing and how it will look, and people are noticing. This guy from work who never spoke to me at school made a comment about how good I looked. I was floored because he'd never said anything to me before. That was a real ego booster!"

SOCIAL WOW: SHARING HERSELF WITH OTHERS

Because Cathy was so afraid of rejection, she spent a lot of extra time on the S.E.L.L. Yourself lessons, learning to gift people with her smile and attention rather than expect anything from them. Once she took the pressure off herself, her fear of being rejected lessened, and the facade began to melt away, allowing the friendlier, softer Cathy to emerge.

"Smiling changed my life. The attention from strangers is most telling. People ask me to participate in more things because I'm more approachable. It's really a shock that people are asking me to step out of my comfort zone more. I'm not sure I like it yet, because I feel more vulnerable, but I'm way out of the box! I hadn't danced since I was ten years old, and now I'm liturgical dancing!

"I even applied the S.E.L.L. techniques at work on one of my students who has been very difficult. It made me realize that charm isn't just for social situations."

SEXUAL WOW: USING SENSUALITY TO PRODUCE SEXUAL ENERGY

Cathy had put her sexuality on the shelf for so long that she'd lost her craving for sex. Much of her work in this unit was geared toward slowly putting her back in touch with her sexual self through her sensuality.

"My most sensual experience while I was enrolled at Stiletto U was simple but still huge for me. I bought myself new sheets and wore a sexy nightgown instead of a T-shirt to bed. It felt great. I felt great, all by myself.

"I'm not in a relationship and sex is still not a part of my life, but it's okay for right now. I still have work to do. I've always been afraid to be more aggressive sexually for fear of rejection, but I'm working up to it.

"I wasn't sure about what I was capable of achieving when I started this, but now I have a better idea—a lot! I learned what to do with positive feedback and how to give positive feedback. I learned that what you say, do, and how you act comes back tenfold and it pays off *huge* to smile! Many things I always knew, but just never did. Stiletto U was an awesome reminder!"

PROFESSOR'S COMMENTS: Cathy came a long way during her semester at Stiletto U. It was amazing to watch her hard, icy exterior melt away, leaving behind a soft, warm, yet still powerful center. Cathy said it best: the key to her transformation was her beginning to care—care more about herself and her appearance, and less about what people might think about her weight. That change of attitude, in tandem with her decision to unleash her dynamic smile onto others, opened up the world to Cathy—a woman who went from describing herself as "funny and quirky" to "engaging and effervescent," from "short and overpowering" to "smiling and getting better with time"! Cathy's disposition changed a hundredfold when she began to feel accepted for being herself.

WHAT SHE KNOWS NOW: Cathy learned to take her innate kindness, compassion, and caring and gift others with it throughout the day. Instead of whining and waiting for others to notice her special qualities, she spent her time noticing theirs, and as she discovered, what goes around comes around! Oh yeah, benevolence is definitely sexy.

WHERE SHE IS NOW: Three years following her graduation, Cathy is still smiling with her eyes. "My life is fuller in a different way now. I'm happier. Everybody used to come before Cathy. No more."

Soon after leaving SU, Cathy enrolled in a weight loss program. She lost some weight before deciding that as long as she was healthy, she was content just the way she was. "I feel good, and I'm still dressing better. I realized that when you care about yourself it changes everything." Cathy is still single and living sensuously. "I'm putting my energy into living every day instead of waiting."

WHEN SEXY HEALS
—GIGI

Gigi, MSA '09
Home: Illinois
Age: 43
Single
Overall Grade: B
Personal Ratings (1–10)
Self-esteem: (4) 6
Feminine Confidence: (0) 2
Sexual Confidence: (0) 1
Social Confidence: (5) 6
Sensual Signatures
Scent: Lavender
Style: Simple elegance
Symbol: Lotus flower
Song: "I'm Beautiful" (Bette Midler)
Charisma: Smart

Moment of Truth: "Realizing that I now love the feeling of being hugged, especially by tall men, which makes me feel enveloped and snug."

What I Want Now: "Inner peace in every moment. I still have a lot that turns in my head."

Gigi had been sexually abused as a child and had lived her entire life immersed in anger, resentment and self-doubt. When she graduated from Stiletto University, she was clearly on a new life path.

The woman who had described herself when she arrived as intense and deep, average and rumpled, left seeing herself as attractive, refined, enthusiastic, and friendly.

"This has been nothing less than transformative. I came to this program scared and with pretty low expectations because of my resistance. The work we did was the spark that led to everything—from better relations at work, to an amazing performance at my commencement ceremony, to deep, deep inner healing work around forgiveness."

Here are some of the highlights from Gigi's semester.

INDIVIDUAL WOW: UNEARTHING HER SENSUALITY

This was a huge unit for Gigi because it was safe and the easiest for her to fully access without interruption by her demons. To her surprise, it also became her key to getting in touch with the beauty and joy existing in the world around her, and gave her a fresh perspective on her life. "This was my favorite part of the course. It was completely grounding and opened me up to a new world. I am now mindful of how glorious touch and smell, in particular, are. I just love the feel of different textures and sensations on my skin, and the smell of lavender that now infuses my home."

When it came to her personal image, Gigi was starting from the ground up. She'd lived so long hiding and trying to remain invisible that she'd never associated clothing with personal style. Gigi started by going through the accessories she already owned, realizing she'd amassed a stunning collection of large, bold bracelets that she rarely wore. She decided to turn them into her signature accessory. Her simple but elegant look evolved throughout the semester, but the real turning point came in this unit when she realized that she'd stopped wearing formless attire and was now sporting figure-skimming clothing that accentuated her slimmed-down figure.

"I love feeling soft, silky clothes next to my body, and I now feel comfortable in my skin in a way I never have before. I feel satisfied with myself as I am. I was looking at someone who had hair of a texture and style that I once coveted. I tried to imagine myself with that hair and realized that I would look ridiculous, and now I wouldn't trade, even if I could. People seem to think that I am regal and commanding in presence. I like how I look."

SOCIAL WOW: REPLACING THE ANGER WITH APPROACHABILITY

After years of remaining socially inhibited, this unit was potentially quite difficult for Gigi. But the feedback she was receiving about her newfound image was helpful in boosting her social confidence. Two things Gigi worked very hard on were smiling with both her mouth and eyes and learning how to graciously receive compliments. "I don't think I scowl as much anymore. I was at a church event and one woman came up to me and said she really liked my energy, and another commented on my 'beaming' smile. I didn't realize that I was smiling so often.

"I love the eye talking; it has had the most resonance for

me. I'd been walking around with dead eyes. It thrills me to enliven through my eyes. It makes such a difference in engaging and connecting with others."

Just learning to smile more made Gigi much more approachable, which naturally led to others feeling more comfortable in her presence. "I now engage very easily in conversation with strangers, and I like the connection. With friends and family, I am just a nicer person overall, more genuinely interested in them and not as angry, so I don't take it out on them."

In addition to smiling and being more approachable, Gigi worked on her ability to receive compliments from other people, particularly men, as a gift and recognition of her inner and outer beauty. A huge turning point came for Gigi when she was walking down the street and a man, very respectfully, complimented her on her figure. She admitted to feeling uncomfortable, but not angry or resentful. This was a major breakthrough.

"Learning another way to perceive compliments from men on the street, rather than the hateful way that I did, and to feel less threatened by them was huge."

SEXUAL WOW: FREEING HER SEXUAL ENERGY

This was understandably the toughest unit for Gigi, and in fact, we reconfigured the lessons to accommodate her sensitivity to the subject. Instead of trying to make her feel more comfortable with sex or a sexy image she'd yet to see in herself, we worked to help Gigi unearth the natural sexual energy that had been deeply buried and intentionally ignored.

"I'd rate my comfort level with my emerging sexual self

as a two out of ten. When it comes to thinking of myself as a sexual woman, the one thing that has changed about my viewpoint is that I can honor my anger, annoyance, and resentful feelings about it, and that's a healthy start.

Defining herself as a woman was one of Gigi's goals. On her final exam she made this statement about her most defining moment as a woman since beginning Stiletto U: "I was walking down the street feeling attractive, doing one of the exercises, imagining how I would feel or act if I looked the way I thought someone very sexy or attractive might look. It was great feeling like that and seeing people respond to it, but really, not caring how people responded because of how I felt."

She adds, "Through this program, I woke up to appreciating and being more alive in the world, and that's a gift worth its weight in gold! It has really helped to significantly transform the remainder of my life, and that's no small thing."

PROFESSOR'S COMMENTS: Gigi was my greatest challenge as a coach, and one of my most rewarding as well. There were many negative layers we had to work our way through. The thickest was her anger. Anger was the emotion she knew best and had made a truce of sorts with because it protected her. Getting through it was tough, but once she began, Gigi really made an effort to change her attitudes by exploring her sensuality. This was a perfect avenue for her because it was inherently safe and instantly gratifying. She slowly began to feel better about herself and became more willing to share her true self with others. More often than not, she walked away feeling confident and empowered, reinforcing the idea that being herself could never be wrong. As

Gigi started letting herself get out and explore the woman she wanted to be, she felt happier, more vibrant, attractive, and lighter in spirit. With happiness taking a more dominant role in her emotional schematic, her anger and resentment lessened enough for her to make some important breakthroughs.

WHAT SHE KNOWS NOW: For a woman most of whose life was devoid of joy, Gigi learned and embraced the fact that pleasure is always accessible. It was just a matter of opening her eyes, ears, nose, mouth, hands, and heart, and reaching out to experience it.

WHERE SHE IS NOW: A few months after completing SU, Gigi felt confident and comfortable enough to drastically change her life. "I accepted a dream job that took me far away from home and my comfort zone. It was all very serendipitous. I feel happy and satisfied about my decision, and I'm still very mindful of my senses and have gotten really comfortable with my body. I'm not hiding it anymore. I'm still not in a relationship. That is an area where I have work to do, but I can see it now. Before, I never thought a relationship would be a part of my life, but it's no longer a black cloud. It will happen when it's right and that is a *huge* step for me. Stiletto U really opened a door of promise that I'm so happy I stepped through!"

CONGRATULATIONS!
YOU HAVE NOW ACCESSED
"THE POWER OF WOW"

Well, here we are at the end of our journey together. I hope that you, like the SU alumni who came before you, are feeling more confident and comfortable in your own skin, and happier and more empowered in your daily life. If you are, you've begun to realize that the true power of WOW is driven by your positive attitude and self-possessed energy, and fueled by sensuous living. Congratulations! Now go out and use that power to make the world a more beautiful place.

I'd love to hear about your Stiletto University experience. Please email me at Stilettou@yahoo.com with your story and final grade and we will email you your Stiletto University diploma.

So, before you turn the last page, throw on your heels, and sashay your confident, sensual self out into the world, I'd like to give you a few last words of advice. Maintaining a solidly sensual attitude and lifestyle doesn't come easy at first, but with mindful application, you'll find it fast becoming the way you do life, as opposed to life simply doing you. Let your semester experience resonate for a while and then go back and revisit whichever classes you need to fully absorb the lesson. Incorporate your sensual signatures into your daily routine so they become a constant reminder to carry yourself as a confident, sensual Stiletto University graduate would. And please, don't get down on yourself if you find yourself temporarily slipping back into your old ways. It takes effort for the happy lessons of sensuous living and loving to become habitual for you and ingrained in your daily routines. Once they are, however, they will forever be at your disposal during the good and bad times.

I want to leave you with some thoughts about butterflies— that iconic symbol of beauty and transformation, and a signature symbol often claimed by Stiletto University students.

It's a natural fact: if you try to help a butterfly emerge from its pupa, it will die. But once it does emerge, it spends its life making love and feasting on nectar. This is yet another vital lesson from Mother Nature: the process of metamorphosis is a solo act that requires dedication, determination, and hard work, but its rewards are most sweet.

And here is a great proverb: "Just when the caterpillar thought the world was over, it became a butterfly." Love it! Translation: Don't give up on securing your sensual self. Just when things seem impossible and you feel like packing up your stilettos, amazing things will happen!

Throughout the semester you've met several of the fabulous SU alumni. You have witnessed where they started upon enrollment in Stiletto University and the life-altering impact living sensuously has made on them since graduation. I want to point out an important advantage that these alumni received: they all had the extra benefit of working individually with me as they worked to unleash their confident, sensual selves. Think of this book, *The Power of WOW*, as your personal guide and touchstone, should you ever need a "refresher course." This coaching is offered to you as well. Check out www.stilettou.com to learn about the available coaching options. You and your friends can also join the SU Study Group and take advantage of our alumni services like teleseminars, Q & A, notification about workshops, events, and other goodies to keep you solidly sensual.

So, until our rose-petal paths meet again, be charming. Be Sexy. Be *you!*

Lori

ABOUT THE AUTHOR

Lori Bryant-Woolridge is an author, sensuality coach, and advocate for healthy, sensual lifestyles. An Emmy-award winning writer, she has written three *Essence* bestselling novels, *Weapons of Mass Seduction: A Novel to Unleash the Sensual You, Read Between the Lies, Hitts & Mrs.*, and is the editor of the popular erotic anthology, *Can't Help The Way That I Feel.* In 2007, she founded Stiletto U, a virtual university designed to teach women how to become the confident, sensual individuals they are meant to be. Lori lives in New Jersey.

Photo by: Marshall Norstein

TO OUR READERS

Viva Editions publishes books that inform, enlighten, and entertain. We do our best to bring you, the reader, quality books that celebrate life, inspire the mind, revive the spirit, and enhance lives all around. Our authors are practical visionaries: people who offer deep wisdom in a hopeful and helpful manner. Viva was launched with an attitude of growth and we want to spread our joy and offer our support and advice where we can to help you live the Viva way: vivaciously!

We're grateful for all our readers and want to keep bringing you books for inspired living. We invite you to write to us with your comments and suggestions, and what you'd like to see more of. You can also sign up for our online newsletter to learn about new titles, author events, and special offers.

Viva Editions
2246 Sixth St.
Berkeley, CA 94710
www.vivaeditions.com
(800) 780-2279
Follow us on Twitter @vivaeditions
Friend/fan us on Facebook